JOURNEY
TO THE
LORD OF POWER

Allah the Generous One, the Raiser of the Dead, the Guardian of All
Existence, the Ever Present.

JOURNEY TO THE LORD OF POWER

A Sufi Manual on Retreat
by
Muhyiddin Ibn 'Arabi

with Notes from a Commentary by 'Abdul-Karim Jili
and an Introduction by Sheikh Muzaffer Ozak al-Jerrahi

Translated by Rabia Terri Harris

Inner Traditions International Ltd.
New York

Inner Traditions International
377 Park Avenue South
New York, NY 10016

Inner Traditions would like to express its appreciation to the
Halveti-Jerrahi Order of America for its help and cooperation in
making this book possible. We would also like to thank Tosun
Bayrak for photographing the calligraphy in this book as well as
kindly providing the translation and the commentary on them.

Library of Congress Cataloging in Publication Data
Ibn al-'Arabi, 1165-1240.
    Journey to the Lord of Power.

    Translation of Risalat al-anwar.
    1. Sufism—Early works to 1800. I. Jili, 'Abd
al-Karim ibn Ibrahim, b. 1365 or 6. Asfar 'an Risalat
al-anwar. English. Selections. 1980. II. Title
BP188.9.I2513   297'.4   81-28
ISBN 0-89281-024-6
ISBN 0-89281-018-1 (Pbk.)

Journey to the Lord of Power is the first in the series of
books on Sufism from the Library of the Halveti-Jerrahi Order of
Dervishes

Typography by Positive Type
Printed in the United States of America

CONTENTS

NOTE ON THE ILLUSTRATIONS

The calligraphy of the "Beautiful Names of Allah," from which the cover is taken, is from the Grand Mosque (Ulu Cami) built in 1399 in Bursa, Turkey. The originals are monumental mural compositions of calligraphy approximately eight feet in height, painted in the nineteenth century by the world-renowed calligrapher Mehmet Shefik.

NOTE ON THE COVER ILLUSTRATION

Also from the Grand Mosque, the cover calligraphy reads *Hu* ("There is no God but He, nothing but He"). *Hu* is Allah's most perfect Name, by which those who see nothing but Allah call upon Him. Those are the "perfect men" who have reached the level of Knowledge of God, the ones who have cleansed their hearts, who have become one with their essence, those who, although their names are still in this world, have annihilated their selves in the flames of Divine Love and moved to the world of unity, the world of God's Eternity.

LIST OF ILLUSTRATIONS

IN THE NAME OF GOD
MOST BENEFICENT, MOST MERCIFUL

TRANSLATOR'S PREFACE

Journey to the Lord of Power, known most widely in Arabic
under the title *Risalat-ul-anwar fima yumnah sahib al-khalwa min
al-asrar* ("Treatise on the Lights in the Secrets Granted One
Who Undertakes Retreat"), by Muhyiddin Ibn ul-'Arabi
(1165-1240), was originally edited in 1204/1205 in Konya,
Turkey. There now exist some seventy manuscript copies in
the libraries of the world, under these titles and such variants
as "The Book of Journey in Reality" and "The Book of
Retreat." There have been two printed editions in Arabic:
Cairo, 1914, and Hyderabad, 1948. This is the work's first
publication in English.

No critical edition of *Journey to the Lord of Power* exists. I
have consulted both printed editions of the text and the partial
seventeenth-century manuscript copy in the Garrett Collection at Princeton University. However, the translation
largely follows a third printed version which accompanies the
commentary.

About the commentary, *al-Isfar 'an risalat-ul-anwar fima
yatajalla li ahl il-dhikr min al-asrar* ("Unveiling of 'Treatise on

the Secrets Revealed to the People of *Dhikr*' '') by 'Abdul-Karim Jili (1365-1408), little information is available. It is undated; bibliographic sources list only two manuscripts. It exists also under the alternate title *Sharh ul-khalwat il-mutlaq* ("Explanation of Absolute Retreat"). The only version available to me was published in Arabic in Damascus in 1929. The selections published here represent the first English language translation of the commentary as well.

Ibn 'Arabi's *Journey to the Lord of Power* was written, as the text makes clear, to answer the questions of an unnamed friend who was himself a saint and Sufi master. Although he produced many volumes, Ibn 'Arabi claimed never to have written anything except in obedience to a divine command. In this letter, he deals with the conditions, experiences, and results of annihilation in God.

Journey to the Lord of Power is a discussion of *khalwa*, spiritual retreat, an advanced and dangerous Sufi practice for the attainment of the Presence of God through absolute abandonment of the world. *Khalwa* is by no means a technique for everyone. Ibn 'Arabi explicitly states that because of the deceptions of the imagination, it may be undertaken only at the order of a shaykh, or by one who has mastered himself. He further points out that to pursue the experiences of *khalwa* without being thoroughly accomplished in the duties and practices of Islam is to invite spiritual destruction. Finally, each stage of the ascent which he describes is a temptation, yielding to which brings calamity and loss. Only one with an overpowering desire for God and no care for anything else is safe in such circumstances.

The practice of *khalwa* in Islam began with the Prophet Muhammad (may Allah's peace and blessings be upon him), who used to retire to a cave in Mount Hira for contemplation. The spiritual ascent through all the degrees of existence to the Divine Presence which Ibn 'Arabi describes also has Prophetic precedent. In the great Night Journey and Ascension, Muhammad was transported—in an instant which was 70,000 years—from Mecca to Jerusalem and from Jerusalem through all the heavens to the Presence of the Beloved, and returned.

There is a tradition that Abu-Jahl, one of the Prophet's major enemies and persecutors, heard reports of this event and went to see Muhammad. The Prophet received him.

"Lift one foot off the ground," Abu-Jahl said.

The Prophet complied.

"Now lift the other," he continued.

"I cannot," answered the Prophet.

"How can you, who cannot even lift your two feet off the ground, claim that you went to the highest heaven last night?" Abu-Jahl demanded.

"Ah, but I didn't say I *went*," the Prophet replied. "I said I was *taken*."

As 'Abdul-Karim Jili points out in his commentary, the gift of this ascension, though given without preparation to the prophets, must be earned by the saints. Its price is the perfection of all the interior and exterior arts of Islam, which means submission to God. Without the knowledge gained through Sacred Law and inner battle with the self, there can be no contemplation, for as Ibn 'Arabi writes:

> Revelation corresponds to the extent and form of knowledge. The knowledge of Him, from Him, that you acquire at the time of your struggle and training you will realize in contemplation later. But what you contemplate of Him will be the form of the knowledge which you established previously. You advance nothing except your transference from knowledge (*'ilm*) to vision (*'ayn*); and the form is one.

Journey to the Lord of Power, in the space of a brief and highly condensed letter, touches on many themes which find their full development only in Ibn 'Arabi's other works. 'Abdul-Karim Jili makes this clear in his commentary, and illuminates many otherwise obscure statements by bringing to bear his deep insight and great familiarity with Ibn 'Arabi's work. His comments on some of the more difficult passages have been appended as notes.

Many stories of Ibn 'Arabi have come down to us. Several of them are related in the Introduction. Much less, however, is known of 'Abdul-Karim Jili. This highly respected man, who died between 1408 and 1417, was also a shaykh, a descendant of the great saint 'Abdul-Qadir Jilani. He is the foremost systematizer and one of the greatest exponents of the work of

TRANSLATOR'S PREFACE

Ibn 'Arabi. His book *al-Insan al-kamil* ("The Perfect Man"), an explanation of Ibn 'Arabi's teachings on the structure of reality and human perfection, is held to be one of the masterpieces of Sufi literature in its own right.

The object of Sufism has been said to be the production of saints. The saints of Islam are called *awliya'*, the friends of God. The Koran describes their state: "the friends of Allah—no fear comes upon them, nor do they grieve" (10:62). The *awliya'* are those in whom no trace of false existence remains. God keeps them continuously in obedience, so that their action is His action. A *hadith qudsi* states, "Nothing is more pleasing to Me, as a means for My servant to draw near to Me, than worship which I have made binding upon him; and My servant does not cease to draw near to Me with added voluntary devotions until I love him; and when I love him I become the hearing with which he hears and the eye with which he sees and the hand with which he grasps and the foot with which he walks." Through the saints, whose life is a testimony to such a state, humanity may understand the work for which it was created, and recognize that the true human being is the representative of God. By divine promise, the world shall not be without them until the end of time.

I would like to acknowledge the assistance of Professor Roy Parviz Mottahedeh of Princeton University and Mr. Simon Bryquer of New York in the revision of the manuscript.

Praise is due to Allah for the generosity of al-Hajj Sheikh

JOURNEY TO THE LORD OF POWER

Muzafferuddin Ozak Efendi al-Jerrahi al-Halveti of Istanbul, whose words provide an enlightening introduction to Ibn 'Arabi's text, and for the invaluable guidance of al-Hajj Sheikh Tosun Bekir Bayrak Efendi al-Jerrahi al-Halveti of New York. I would like to dedicate this translation to my father and my mother.

Any errors that are in this book are mine; the praise is His. May the reader find his reading profitable.

Rabia Terri Harris

INTRODUCTION

by

Sheikh Muzaffer Ozak al-Jerrahi

This treatise, which contains divine mysteries, is an
illuminating guide for seekers of truth and vision. Those who
wish to be intimates of God, who stroll in the garden looking
for the rosebuds of inner knowledge, should read this book
and learn to "be." Since the author of this work is Ibn 'Arabi,
whoever browses through its words will be conversing with
him.

The miraculous spiritual influence of this saint, in the East
and in the West, is brilliantly clear. He has taught mankind
tawhid, Unity, and will continue enlightening it until the Day
of Last Judgment. His teaching of the wonder of Creation and
his miraculous knowledge—displayed in such books as *al-
Futuhat al-Makkiyya* ("Meccan Revelations"), *Fusus al-hikam*
("Bezels of Wisdom"), and many others, numbering over
500—bear witness to his importance.

He had as many enemies as people who loved him, bigots
who like bats were blinded by the light of the saint. Some men
become enemies of those they do not know, cannot know, and

cannot understand. Even the ones who named him *al-shaykh al-akbar* (''the Greatest Shaykh'') were among those who did not understand him. Some of them even hated him. The saint not only forgave these deficient people but declared that he would intercede on their behalf on the Day of Last Judgment, for they were to be pitied for not having been able to comprehend him. Certainly, just as the goldsmith knows the value of gold, the wise know the value of knowledge and the all-knowing Perfect Man forgives the ignorant their poverty. This compassion of the saint is sufficient proof of his perfection.

One day, one of Ibn 'Arabi's opponents was taken sick. The shaykh went to visit him. He knocked on the door and begged the sick man's wife to announce that he wished to pay his respects. The woman took the message and, returning, told the shaykh that her husband did not wish to see him. The shaykh had no business in this house, she informed him. The proper place for him was the church. The shaykh thanked the woman and said that since a good man like her husband would certainly not send him to a bad place, he would comply with the suggestion. So after praying for the health and welfare of the sick man, the shaykh departed for the church.

When he arrived, he removed his shoes, entered with humble courtesy, and slowly and silently headed toward a corner, where he sat down. The priest was in the midst of delivering a sermon to which Ibn 'Arabi listened with the utmost attention. During the sermon, the shaykh felt that the priest had slandered Jesus by attributing to him the claim that

INTRODUCTION

he was the son of God. The shaykh stood up and courteously objected to this statement. "O venerable priest," he began, "Holy Jesus did not say that. On the contrary, he foretold the good news of the arrival of the Prophet Ahmad (Muhammad, peace and blessings be upon him)."

The priest denied that Jesus had said this. The debate went on and on. Finally the shaykh, pointing to the image of Jesus on the church wall, told the priest to ask Jesus himself. He would answer and decide the issue once and for all. The priest protested vehemently, pointing out that a picture could not speak. This picture would, insisted the shaykh, for God, who had made Jesus speak while a baby in the arms of the Holy Virgin, was able to make his picture speak as well. The congregation following the heated debate became excited at this statement. The priest was forced to turn to the image of Jesus and address it: "O Son of God! Show us the true path. Tell us which of us is right in our claim." With God's Will, the picture spoke and answered: "I am not the son of God, I am His messenger, and after me came the last of the prophets, the Holy Ahmad; I foretold that to you, and I repeat this good news now."

With this miracle, the whole congregation accepted Islam and, with Ibn 'Arabi leading them, marched through the streets to the mosque. As they passed by the house of the sick man, he could be seen within, his eyes wide open in astonishment, looking out of the window at this curious sight. The saint stopped, and blessed and thanked the man who had insulted him, saying that he was to be praised for the salvation of all these people.

Not many people understood the saint during his lifetime. One day he went up the mountain in Damascus where he preached, and said: "People of Damascus, the god which you worship is under my feet."

On hearing these words, the people jailed him, and were prepared to kill him. In fact, according to one tradition, at that incident he was martyred. According to another tradition, a shaykh of his time, Abul-Hassan, mitigated his words and saved him from death with the following dialogue:

"How could people imprison someone," he asked Ibn 'Arabi, "through whom the world of angels came to the mortal world?"

"My words were spoken," the shaykh replied, "through the intoxication of the state you describe."

Yet Ibn 'Arabi's words and his works created such a violent reaction in his time that the people destroyed his tomb after his death without leaving any trace of it.

One of his many enigmatic statements was *"Idha dakhala al-sin ila al-shin / yazhara qabru Muhyiddin,"* which means: "When *S* will enter *SH* [the letters *sin* and *shin* in Arabic], the tomb of Muhyiddin will be discovered." When the ninth Ottoman sultan, Selim II, conquered Damascus in 1516, he learned of this statement from a contemporary scholar named Zembilli Ali Efendi, who interpreted it as a prophecy which meant: "When Selim [whose name starts with the letter *sin*] enters the

INTRODUCTION

city of Sham [the Arabic name of Damascus, which begins
with the letter *shin*], he will discover Ibn 'Arabi's tomb.'' So
Sultan Selim found out from the theologians of the city the
place where the saint had made the declaration ''The god
which you worship is under my feet,'' and had it excavated.
First he uncovered a treasure of gold coins, which revealed
what the saint had meant. Nearby he discovered his tomb.
With the treasure he found, Sultan Selim built a magnificent
shrine and mosque on the site of the tomb. It still stands today
in the city of Damascus and is found at a place called Salihiyya
on the slopes of the mountain Qasiyun.

Muhibbuddin al-Tabari* attributes the following story to
his mother:

Muhyiddin Ibn 'Arabi was delivering a sermon at the
Kaaba on the meaning of the Kaaba. Inwardly, I
disagreed with his teaching. That night I saw the shaykh
in my dream. In this dream, Fakhruddin al-Razi, one of
the greatest theologians of the time, came to the
Pilgrimage with great pomp and ceremony, and was
circumambulating the Kaaba. His eyes fell on a simple
man in his pilgrim's shroud who was sitting there
quietly. He said to himself: ''The insolence of this man,
not to stand in the presence of a great man like me!'' A
little while later, he came to preach in the Grand

*See Glossary.

11

Mosque in Mecca. The whole population of the Holy City had gathered to hear the words of this great scholar who was the author of the most important interpretation of the Koran. Fakhruddin al-Razi slowly mounted the pulpit and began, "O great congregation of Muslims"—and nothing else came out of his mouth. It was as though all the contents of his mind had been erased. He began to sweat with embarrassment. He excused himself, saying he was not feeling well, and left the pulpit without a word. When he reached home, he protested and prayed, "O Lord, what have I done that you should punish me with such embarrassment?" That night in a dream he was shown the man whom he had secretly reproached for not standing in his presence. It was Muhyiddin Ibn 'Arabi. For days he searched for him everywhere. Just as he had given up hope of finding him, there was a knock at the door, and Ibn 'Arabi was standing in front of him. He asked for forgiveness, and his knowledge was returned to him.

In recent times, there was the case of another scholar, Ibrahim Haleri, the imam of the Fatih Mosque in Istanbul, an extremely orthodox man who opposed the religious teachings of Ibn 'Arabi. One day in heated discussion with people who defended the shaykh, he stamped his foot, saying, "If I could have been there, I would have crushed his head like that!" In so doing, he stepped on a huge nail. The wound never healed, causing his death. (The Fatih Mosque has a stone, not a wooden, floor.)

According to an oral tradition, one day in Damascus Ibn 'Arabi saw a beautiful young Jewish boy. As he looked upon him, the boy came to him and addressed him as "father." From that day on the boy never left him. The father of the boy searched, found him with the shaykh, and wanted to take him away. The boy did not recognize him and claimed that the shaykh was his father. The father, in amazement, told the shaykh that he could bring hundreds of witnesses to prove that the boy was his son. The shaykh responded, "If the boy claims that I am his father, then I am his father." The father went to court claiming his boy, showing hundreds of witnesses. When the judge asked the shaykh if the boy was his, the shaykh demanded that the boy be asked. The boy claimed the shaykh as his father. Then the shaykh asked the witnesses if this Jewish boy had memorized the Koran. They answered, "How could a Jewish boy memorize the Koran?" The judge asked the boy to recite the Koran, which he did with great skill and beauty. Then the shaykh asked the witnesses if the boy knew the traditions of the Prophet Muhammad. They answered, "How could a Jewish boy know such a science, which does not belong to his way of life?" The judge closely questioned the boy about Prophetic traditions. The boy answered his every question correctly and completely. The Jews who understood this miracle accepted Islam.

The following story is included toward the end of the

Futuhat al-Makkiyya: In the orthodox atmosphere of a school of canonic law, a teacher was explaining the root of the word for heretic *(zindiq)*. Some mischievous students wondered if perhaps it came from the word *zenuddin,* which means "religious woman." Another mischievous student said, *"Zindiq* is someone like Muhyiddin Ibn 'Arabi. . . isn't that so, Master?" The teacher curtly answered yes.

It was Ramadan, the Month of Fasting, and the teacher had invited the students back to his house to break the fast with him. Sitting and waiting for the meal to start, the same mischievous students teased their teacher, saying, "If you cannot reveal to us the name of the greatest saint of our time, we will not break our fast with your food." The teacher answered that the greatest shaykh of all times was Muhyiddin Ibn 'Arabi. The students protested, saying that earlier at school when they had given Ibn 'Arabi as an example of a heretic, he had agreed. Now he claimed that the shaykh was the greatest saint of their times! The teacher answered, a hint of a smile about his lips: "At the school we are among men of orthodoxy, scholars and legists; here we are among men of love."

GLIMPSES OF
THE LIFE OF IBN 'ARABI

by

Tosun Bayrak al-Jerrahi

Ibn 'Arabi's father, 'Ali ibn Muhammad ibn 'Arabi, went to Baghdad at an advanced age. His dearest wish was to leave a son in his place when he passed away. He went to see the great shaykh Muhyiddin 'Abdul-Qadir Jilani and asked him to pray for God to give him the gift of a son. The shaykh secluded himself and went into deep contemplation. On his return, he informed 'Ali ibn Muhammad: ''I have looked into the world of secrets and it has been revealed to me that you will have no descendants, so do not tire yourself out trying.''

Although crestfallen, the old man would not give up. He begged and insisted: ''O Saint, God will certainly grant your prayers. I ask you to intervene in this matter for me.''

Shaykh 'Abdul-Qadir Jilani once again withdrew and fell into deep contemplation. After a while he came back and said that although 'Ali ibn Muhammad was not destined to have a

15

descendant, the saint himself was so destined. Would the old man like to have the saint's future son?

His visitor gladly accepted. The two men stood back to back, their arms interlocked. 'Ali ibn Muhammad later recounted this incident:

"When I was back to back with the saint 'Abdul-Qadir Jilani, I felt something warm running down from my neck to the small of my back. After a while a son was born to me, and I named him Muhyiddin, as 'Abdul-Qadir Jilani had ordered."

Muhyiddin Ibn 'Arabi's full name was Abu-Bakr Muhammad ibn 'Ali ibn Muhammad al-Hatimi al-Ta'i al-Andalusi. He has been given many titles: *al-shaykh al-akbar,* the Greatest Shaykh; *khatim al-awliya' al-Muhammadi,* the Seal of the Saints of Muhammad; *al-shaykh al-a'zam,* the Exalted Shaykh; *qutb al-'arifin,* Axis of True Knowledge; *imam ul-munahiyuddin,* Religious Leader of the Converts; *rahbar ul-'alam,* Guide of the World; and many more. On his great learning, Ibn Jawziya has commented, "Ibn 'Arabi was well versed in alchemy, and knew the secret of the Greatest Name of God, which is hidden in the Koran." Shaykh Sa'duddin Hamawi* said, "Muhyiddin is an ocean of knowledge which has no shores."

Muhyiddin Ibn 'Arabi was born in the city of Murcia in the then Islamic province of Andalusia, Spain, on Monday the 17th of the holy month of Ramadan in the year 560 A.H. (July 28, 1165). His father was a Sufi and a renowned and respected

*See Glossary.

person. In his early childhood, he was recognized and taught by two women saints, Yasmin of Marchena and Fatima of Córdoba. At the age of eight, Ibn 'Arabi and his family moved to Seville where he studied with Abu-Muhammad and Ibn Bashkuwal, two of the greatest theologians and scholars of the Prophetic Traditions of the time. By the time he was nineteen years old, his father's friend, the famous philosopher and mystic Ibn Rushd (known to the West as Averroës), expressed an interest in meeting him. Much moved by the intense power which he felt through exchanging only a few words with the young man, the scholar spoke to his father in terms which Ibn 'Arabi recalled as follows:

> He thanked God to have been able to meet someone who had entered into spiritual retreat ignorant and left it as I had. He said: "It was a case whose possibility I had affirmed without encountering anyone who had experienced it. Glory be to God that I have lived at a time when there exists a master of this experience, one of those who opens the locks of His doors. Glory be to God to have granted me the gift of seeing one of them myself.

Since it had been the rumor of "what God had revealed to the young man in the course of his spiritual retreat" which had attracted the attention of Ibn Rushd, we know that Ibn 'Arabi had his first experience with the subject of this book, the mystical ascent in *khalwa*, while still less than twenty years old. He did not write *Journey to the Lord of Power*, however, for another twenty years.

In 1201, at the age of thirty-six, Ibn 'Arabi traveled to Mecca for the Pilgrimage. At that time he prayed for God to reveal to him all that was to happen in the material and spiritual worlds. God, accepting his wish, opened the world of secrets to him. Concerning these matters, Ibn 'Arabi later commented: "I know the name and genealogy of every *qutb* who will come until the Day of Judgment. But since to oppose what is destined is sure destruction, from compassion for future generations I have decided to hide this knowledge."

After the Pilgrimage, Ibn 'Arabi traveled in Egypt, Iraq, and Damascus, and stopped in Konya, Turkey, where he met Sadruddin Qunyawi, a young Sufi scholar, whose mother he married. The young Sadruddin became one of his closest disciples, whom he enriched with great material and spiritual knowledge. *Journey to the Lord of Power*, edited in Konya by the author three years after his Pilgrimage, was probably originally addressed to this holy man.

In the year 1223, Ibn 'Arabi returned to Damascus, where he met, visibly and invisibly, with many other Sufi masters. There he spent the rest of his life. He is believed to have died in 1240.

Ibn 'Arabi mentions that he met Khidr, the hidden guide of the Sufis, three times. His first meeting he recounts in the following manner:

GLIMPSES OF THE LIFE OF IBN 'ARABI

It was early in my education. My shaykh, Abul Hassan, attributed some knowledge to someone. That whole day I continuously disagreed with him about it. When I left him, while returning to my house I met a beautiful person who greeted me and said, "The things that your teacher told you were right—accept them." I ran back to my shaykh and told him what had happened. He told me that he had prayed to have Khidr come and affirm his teaching. On hearing that, I once and for all decided never to disagree again.

Of his second meeting he says:

...I was in the port of Tunisia on board a ship. I couldn't sleep one night and went strolling on the deck. I was watching a beautiful full moon, when suddenly I saw a tall, white-bearded man coming toward me, walking on water alongside the ship. I was astonished. He came right in front of me and put his right foot on his left foot in salutation. I saw that his feet were not wet. He greeted me, said a few words, and started toward the city of Menares, which was on a hill nearby. To my amazement he traveled a mile with each step he took. From afar I could hear his beautiful voice chanting the *dhikr*. The next day I went to the city, where I met a shaykh who asked me how my evening meeting with Khidr had been and what we had talked about.

Ibn 'Arabi's third meeting with Khidr, according to one tradition, took place in a little mosque on the shores of the Atlantic in Spain where Ibn 'Arabi was making his noon prayers. He had someone accompanying him who denied the existence of miracles. There were a few other travelers in the mosque. Suddenly he saw among them the same being whom he had previously seen in Tunisia. The tall, white-bearded man took his straw prayer mat from the prayer niche, rose fourteen feet into the air, and made his prayer from there. Later he came back to tell Ibn 'Arabi that he had done this as a demonstration for the skeptic in his company who had denied miracles.

When Muhyiddin Ibn 'Arabi evolved above the level of Shaykh Abul-Hassan al-'Uryani, he wrote a letter to his teacher, saying, "Turn toward me with your heart and ask me your questions, and I will turn toward you with my heart and answer them."

After a while he received a letter from his teacher, which said:

> I dreamed that all the saints were gathered in a circle with two men in the center. One of them was Abul-Hassan ibn Siban. I could not see the face of the other. Then I heard a voice saying that the other man in the center was an Andalusian, and that one of the two would be the *qutb* of our time. A verse from the Koran was chanted and both of them prostrated themselves,

and the voice said, "Whoever lifts his head first will be the *qutb.*" The Andalusian lifted his head first. I asked the voice a question without letters or words. The voice answered me by blowing in my direction. This breath contained the answers to all my questions. Both I and all the saints in the circle went into ecstasy with this breath. I looked at the face of the Andalusian in the center of the circle. It was you, O Muhyiddin Ibn 'Arabi.

JOURNEY
TO THE
LORD OF POWER

IN THE NAME OF GOD
MOST BENEFICENT, MOST MERCIFUL

Praise is due to God, the Giver and Originator of Reason, Ordainer and Institutor of the Transmission. His are the grace and the might; from Him are the power and the strength. There is no God save He, Lord of the Tremendous Throne. And may the peace and blessings of God be upon him in whom are established the signs of guidance, whom He sent with the light by which He guides—and misleads—whom He wills; and upon his noble family and pure companions, until the Day of Judgment.

I shall answer your question, O noble friend and intimate companion, concerning the Journey to the Lord of Power (may He be exalted) and the arrival in His presence, and the return, through Him, from Him to His Creation, without separation. Certainly there is nothing in existence except God Most High, His attributes, and His actions. Everything is He, and of Him and from Him and to Him. If He were to be veiled from the world for the blink of an eye, the world would vanish at one stroke; it only remains through His preserving and watching over it. However, His appearance in His light is so intense that it overpowers our perceptions, so that we call His manifestation a veil.

I shall first describe (may Allah grant you success) the nature of the journey to Him, then the procedure of arriving and standing before Him, and what He says to you as you sit on the carpet of His vision. Then the nature of the return from Him to the presence (*hadra*) of His actions: with Him and to Him. And I shall describe absorption in Him, which is a station less than the station of return.[1]

Know, O noble brother, that while the paths are many, the Way of Truth is single. The seekers of the Way of Truth are individuals. So although the Way of Truth is one, the aspects it presents vary with the varying conditions of its seekers; with the balance or imbalance of the seeker's constitution, the persistence or absence of his motivation, the strength or weakness of his spiritual nature, the straightness or deviation of his aspiration, the health or illness of his relation to his goal. Some seekers possess all of the favorable characteristics, while others possess only some. Thus we see that the seeker's constitution, for instance, may be a hindrance, while his spiritual striving may be noble and good. And this principle applies in all cases.

I must first make clear to you the knowledge of the matrices of Realms, and what those Realms imply in this place. The Realms (*mawatin*) is a term for the substrata of the moments in which things come to exist and experience actually occurs. It is necessary that you know what the Truth wants from you in any Realm, so that you hasten to it without hesitation and without resistance.[2]

The Realms, although they are many, are all derived from six. The first Realm is [the pre-existence in which we were asked the question] "Am I not your Lord?" Our physical existence has removed us from this Realm. The second Realm is the world we are now in. The third Realm is the Interval through which we travel after the lesser and greater deaths. The fourth Realm is the Resurrection on the awakening earth and the return to the original condition. The fifth Realm is the Garden and the Fire. The sixth Realm is the Sand Dune outside the Garden. And in each of these Realms are places which are Realms within Realms, and the realization of them in their multiplicity is not within human power.[3]

In our situation we only need an explanation of the Realm of this world, which is the place of responsibilty, trial, and works.

Know that since God created human beings and brought them out of nothingness into existence, they have not stopped being travelers. They have no resting place from their journey except in the Garden or the Fire, and each Garden and Fire is in accordance with the measure of its people. Every rational person must know that the journey is based upon toil and the hardships of life, on afflictions and tests and the acceptance of dangers and very great terrors. It is not possible for the traveler to find in this journey unimpaired comfort, security, or bliss.

For waters are variously flavored and weather changes, and the character of the people at every place where one stops differs from their character at the next. The traveler needs to learn what is useful from each situation. He is the companion of each one for a night or an hour, and then departs. How could ease be reasonably expected by someone in this condition?

We have not mentioned this to answer the people fond of comfort in this world, who strive for it and are devoted to the collection of worldly rubble. We do not occupy ourselves with or turn our attention to those engaged in this petty and contemptible activity. But we mention it as counsel to whoever wishes to hasten the bliss of contemplation in other than its given Realm, and to hasten the state of *fana'*, annihilation, elsewhere than in its native place, and who desires absorption in the Real by means of obliteration from the worlds.[4]

The masters among us are scornful of this [ambition] because it is a waste of time and a loss of [true] rank, and associates the Realm with that which is unsuitable to it.[5] For the world is the King's prison, not His house; and whoever seeks the King in His prison, without departing from it entirely, violates the rule of right behavior (*adab*), and something of great import escapes him. For the time of *fana'* in the Truth is the time of the abandonment of a station higher than the one attained.

Revelation corresponds to the extent and form of knowledge. The knowledge of Him, from Him, that you acquire at the time of your struggle and training you will realize in contemplation later. But what you contemplate of Him will be the form of the knowledge which you established previously. You advance nothing except your transference from knowledge ('ilm) to vision ('ayn); and the form is one.

[In contemplation] you obtain that which you ought to have left to its proper Realm, and that is the House of the Other World in which there is no labor. So it would be better for you if, at the time of your contemplation, you were engaged in labor outwardly, and at the same time in the reception of knowledge from God inwardly. You would then increase virtue and beauty in your spiritual nature, which seeks its Lord through knowledge received from Him through works and piety, and also in your personal nature, which seeks its paradise. For the human subtle nature is resurrected in the form of its knowledge, and the bodies are resurrected in the form of their works, either in beauty or in ugliness.

So it is until the last breath, when you are separated from the world of obligation and the Realm of ascending paths and progressive development. And only then will you harvest the fruit which you have planted.

If you have understood all of this, then know (may God grant success to us both) that if you want to enter the presence of the Truth and receive from Him without intermediary, and you desire intimacy with Him, this will not be appropriate as long as your heart acknowledges any lordship other than His. For you belong to that which exercises its authority over you.

Of this there is no doubt. And seclusion from people will become inevitable for you, and preference for retreat (*khalwa*)[6] over human associations, for the extent of your distance from creation is the extent of your closeness to God—outwardly and inwardly.

Your first duty is to search for the knowledge which establishes your ablution and prayer, your fasting and reverence. You are not obliged to seek out more than this. This is the first door of the journey; then work; then moral heedfulness; then asceticism; then trust. And in the first of the states of trust, four miracles befall you. These are signs and evidences of your attainment of the first degree of trust. These signs are crossing the earth, walking on water, traversing the air, and being fed by the universe. And that is the reality within this door. After that, stations and states and miracles and revelations come to you continuously until death.

And for God's sake, do not enter retreat until you know what your station is, and know your strength in respect to the power of imagination. For if your imagination rules you, then there is no road to retreat except by the hand of the shaykh who is discriminating and aware. If your imagination is under control, then enter retreat without fear.

Discipline is incumbent upon you before the retreat. Spiritual discipline (*riyada*) means training of character, abandonment of heedlessness, and endurance of indignities. For if a person begins before he has acquired discipline, he will never become a man, except in a rare case.

JOURNEY TO THE LORD OF POWER

When you withdraw from the world, beware of people coming to see you and approaching you, for he who withdraws from the people does not open his door to their visits. Indeed the object of seclusion is the departure from people and their society, and the object of departure from people is not leaving their physical company, but rather that neither your heart nor your ear should be a receptacle for the superfluous words they bring. Your heart will not become clear of the mad ravings of the world except by distance from them. And everyone who "withdraws" in his house and opens the door to people visiting him is a seeker of leadership and esteem, driven from the door of God Most High; and for someone like this, destruction is closer than the shoelace of his shoe. For God's sake, for God's sake, protect yourself from the deceit of the ego in this station, for most of the world is destroyed by it. So shut your door against the world; and thus the door of your house will be between you and your people.

And occupy youself with *dhikr*, remembrance of God, with whatever sort of *dhikr* you choose. The highest of them is the Greatest Name; it is your saying "Allah, Allah," and nothing beyond "Allah."

Protect yourself from the misfortunes of corrupt imaginings that distract you from remembrance. Be careful of your diet. It is better if your food be nourishing but devoid of animal fat.[7] Beware of satiation and excessive hunger. Keep your constitution in balance, for if dryness is excessive, it leads to corrupt imaginings and long, delirious ravings.

31

If there should be an influence which alters the constitution[8]—and that is desirable—distinguish between angelic and demonic spiritual influences by what you find in yourself when they come to an end. That is, if the influence is angelic, it is followed by coolness and bliss. You will not be aware of any pain; you will not undergo any alteration of form;[9] and the influence leaves knowledge. But if it is demonic, physical disorientation, pain and distress, bewilderment and vileness ensue; and it leaves mental disorder. Protect yourself, and do not cease repeating the *dhikr* in your heart, until God drives the demonic influence from it.[10] That is what the situation calls for.

Be sure that you articulate what you intend. Let your covenant at your entry into retreat be that there is nothing like unto God. And to each form that appears to you in retreat and says "I am God," say: "Far exalted be God above that! You are *through* God." Remember the form of what you saw. Turn your attention from it and occupy yourself with *dhikr* continually.

This is one covenant. The second one is that you will not seek from Him in retreat anything other than Himself and that you will not attach your *himma,* the power of the heart's intention, to anything other than Him. And if everything in the universe should be spread before you, receive it graciously—but do not stop there. Persist in your quest, for He is testing you. If you stay with what is offered, He will escape you. But if you attain Him, nothing will escape you.

He is Allah besides whom there is no God, the Beneficent, the Merciful, the King who owns and rules the universe, the Pure devoid of all errors, weaknesses, shortcomings and heedlessness, the Granter of total security, the Author of Peace.

If you know this, then know that God tests you through what He spreads before you. What He first discloses to you is His gift of command over the material order, as I shall discuss. It is the unveiling of the sensory world which is hidden from you, so that walls and shadows do not veil you from what people are doing in their houses. However, if God has informed you of anyone's secret, you are obliged to preserve it from exposure. For if you were to expose it and say this one is a fornicator and this one a drunkard and this one a slanderer and this one a thief, you yourself would be the greater sinner and indeed Satan would have entered into you. So act in accordance with the Divine Name al-Sattar, the Veiler. And if this person were to come to you, warn him privately about his actions and counsel him to have shame before God and not to transgress God's limits. Turn away from this type of perception as much as possible, and occupy yourself with dhikr.

We shall explain [the means of telling] the difference between sensory and imaginational subtle perception. That is, when you see someone's form or some created action, if you close your eyes and the perception remains with you, it is in your imagination; but if it is hidden from you, then your consciousness of it is attached to the place in which you saw it. [If it is perception of the latter kind] when you turn your attention away from it and occupy yourself with dhikr, you will move from the sensory to the imaginal level.

And there descend upon you abstract intelligible ideas in

sensory forms. This descent is difficult, since no one knows what is meant by these forms except a prophet, or whomever God wills among the righteous. So do not concern yourself with this. If you are offered something to drink, choose water. If there is no water among the offerings, choose milk. And if both of them are presented to you, combine the water and the milk. This also applies to honey: Drink it. Be careful of drinking wine unless it is mixed with rainwater. Refrain from drinking it otherwise, even if it is mixed with the water of rivers and springs.[11] Occupy yourself with *dhikr* until the world of imagination is lifted from you and the world of abstract meanings free of matter is revealed to you.

Occupy yourself with *dhikr,* remembrance, until the Remembered manifests Himself to you and calling Him to memory is effaced in the actual recollection of Him. However, this [vanishing of *dhikr*] is the essence not only of contemplation but also of sleep. The way to distinguish between them is that contemplation leaves its evidence and is followed by bliss, whereas sleep leaves nothing and is followed, on awakening, by remorse and the asking of forgiveness.

Then Almighty God spreads before you the degrees of the kingdom as a test. This is appointed to you as an obligation.

First you will discover the secrets of the mineral world. You will become acquainted with the secret of every stone and its particular harmful and beneficial qualities. If you become enamored of this world, it will trap you, and you will be exiled

Light upon light. Allah guides to His light whom He pleases
[Koran 24:35].

from God. He will strip you of everything you held on to, and you will be lost. But if you let go and occupy yourself with *dhikr* and take refuge at the side of the Remembered, then He will free you from that mode and unveil the vegetal world. Every green thing will call out to you its harmful and beneficial qualities. Let your judgment be what it was before. At the time of the unveiling of the mineral world let your nourishment be what increases heat and moisture, and at the unveiling of the vegetal world let it be what balances heat and moisture.

And if you do not stop, He will reveal the animal world to you. [The animals] will greet you and acquaint you with their harmful and beneficial qualities. Every sort of creature will acquaint you with its proclamation of majesty and praise. Pay attention to this: If you become aware of all these worlds as engaged in the same *dhikr* which occupies you, your perception is imaginational, not real. It is your own state which is called up for you in all existent things. But when you witness in them the varieties of their own *dhikr,* that is sound perception. This ascent is the ascent of dissolution of the order of nature, and the state of contraction (*qabd*) will accompany you in these worlds.[12]

Then after this, He reveals to you the infusion of the world of life-force into lives, and what influences this has in every being according to its predisposition, and how the expressions [of faith] are included in this infusion.[13]

And if you do not stop with this, He reveals to you the "surface signs."[14] You will be admonished with terrors, and many sorts of states will befall you. You will see clearly the apparatus of transformations: how the dense becomes subtle and the subtle dense. And if you do not stop with this, the light of the scattering of sparks will become visible to you, and there will be a need to veil yourself from it. Do not be afraid, and persevere in the *dhikr*, for if you persevere in the *dhikr*, disaster will not overcome you.

If you do not stop with this, He reveals to you the light of the ascendant stars[15] and the form of the universal order.[16] And you will see directly the *adab*, the proper conduct, for entering the Divine Presence and the *adab* for standing before the Real and the *adab* for leaving His presence for Creation; and the perpetual contemplation by the different aspects of the Divine Names (*al-asma' al-ilahiyya*) "the Manifest" and "the Hidden"; and the Perfection of which not everyone becomes aware. For all that passes away from the aspect of the Manifest comes under the aspect of the Hidden. The essence is one. Nothing has passed away.

And after this, you will know the means of receiving divine knowledge from God Most High, and how one must prepare oneself for its reception. So know the proper conduct of receiving and giving, contraction and expansion; and how to protect the heart, which is the place of the arrival of states, from burning destruction; and that all the ways are circles. There is no straight line. This letter is too brief to deal with matters like these.

And if you do not stop with this, He reveals to you the

The One who plans and rules the universe and all that happens therein. The generous Pardoner of repentant sinners, the Benefactor without conditions.

degrees of speculative sciences, sound integral ideas, and the forms of perplexing questions which confuse understanding. He reveals the difference between supposition and knowledge, the birth of possibilities between the world of spirits and the physical world,[17] the cause of that genesis, the infusion of the Divine Mystery into the domain of His loving concern,[18] the cause of abandoning the world by effort or otherwise— and other related matters which require long explanations.

And if you do not stop with all of this, He reveals to you the world of formation and adornment and beauty, what is proper for the intellect to dwell upon from among the holy forms, the vital breathings from beauty of form and harmony, and the overflow of languour and tenderness and mercy in all things characterized by them. And from this level comes the sustenance of poets, while from the one before comes the sustenance of preachers.

And if you do not stop with this, He reveals to you the degrees of the *qutb*. All that you witnessed before is from the world of the left hand, not from the world of the right hand. And this is the place of the heart. If He manifests this world to you, you will know the reflections, and the endlessness of endlessnesses, and the eternity of eternities, and the order of existences and how being is infused into them. You are given the divine wisdoms and the power to preserve them and integrity to transmit them to the wise, and you are given the power of symbols and a view of the whole, and authority over the veil and the unveiling.

And if you do not stop with this, He reveals to you the world of fever and rage and zeal for truth and falsehood; the foundation of apparent difference in the world, the variation of forms, discord and hatred. And if you do not stop with this, He reveals to you the world of jealousy and the unveiling of the Truth before the more perfect of His faces; sound opinions, true schools, and revealed traditions; and you will see as a knower that God Most High has adorned them, among the holy knowledges, with the most beautiful adornments. And there is nothing that pertains to a station which He reveals to you that does not greet you with honor, reverence, and exaltation; its degree of the Divine Presence is made clear to you, and [each one] loves you in its essence.[19]

And if you do not stop with this, He reveals to you the world of dignity and serenity and firmness; the ruse (*makr*), the enigmas and the secrets, and other matters of that sort. And if you do not stop with this, He reveals to you the world of bewilderment and helplessness and inability and the treasuries of works; and this is the highest heaven.[20]

And if you do not stop with this, He reveals to you the Gardens: the degrees of their ascending steps, their blending into one another, and how they compare to one another in their pleasure. And you are stopped on the narrow path and brought to the brink of Hell, and look down upon the degrees of its descending steps, how they blend into one another and how they compare to one another in their rigor. He reveals to you the works connected to each of these two abodes. And if

Allah the Ever-Living One, the Owner of all knowledge and power, the Self-Sustaining by whom all subsists, the All-Pervasive, the Only One, without partner or likeness.

you do not stop with this, He reveals one of the sanctuaries where spirits are absorbed in the Divine Vision. In it they are drunken and bewildered. The power of ecstasy has conquered them, and their state beckons you.

And if you do not stop with this beckoning, a light is revealed in which you do not see anything other than yourself. In it a great rapture and deep transport of love seizes you, and in it you find bliss with God that you have not known before. All that you saw previously becomes small in your eyes, and you sway like a lamp.[21]

And if you do not stop with this, He reveals the [original] forms of the sons of Adam. And veils are lifted. And veils descend.[22] And they have a special praise which upon hearing you recognize, and you are not overcome.[23] You see your form among them, and from it you recognize the moment which you are in.

And if you do not stop with this, He reveals to you the Throne of Mercy (*sarir al-rahmaniyya*). Everything is upon it. If you regard everything you will see the totality of what you knew in it, and more than this: no world or essence remains that you do not witness there. Search for yourself in everything: If it is appropriate, you will know your destination and place and the limit of your degree, and which Divine Name is your Lord and where your portion of gnosis and sainthood exist—the form of your uniqueness.

And if you do not stop with this, He reveals to you the Pen, the First Intellect, the master and teacher of everything. You examine its tracing and know the message it bears and witness its inversion, and its reception and particularization of the comprehensive [knowledge] from the angel al-Nuni.[24]

And if you do not stop with this, He reveals the Mover of the Pen, the right hand of the Truth.[25]

And if you do not stop with this, you are eradicated,[26] then withdrawn,[27] then effaced, then crushed,[28] then obliterated.

When the effects of eradication and what follows are terminated, you are affirmed,[29] then made present, then made to remain, then gathered together, then assigned. And the robes of honor which [your degree] requires are conferred upon you, and they are many.

Then you return to your path and examine all that you saw in different forms until you return to the world of your limited earthly senses. Or [you will hold fast] there where you were absent; and the destination of every seeker depends upon the road which he traveled.

Among [the ones who complete this journey] are those entrusted with His Word, and among them are those not entrusted with His Word. And whoever is entrusted with a Word, no matter which Word it is, becomes the inheritor of the prophet of that language.* This is what is referred to by the

---

*Each prophet manifests a particular aspect of the divine discourse, and "speaks" in the "language" of that aspect, embodying a Word. The saints who realize these perfect relationships are thus

Allah, may His glory be exalted. (Allah, the word of glory (*lafz al-jelal*), is the personal name (*ism al-dhat*) of God, the name of His essence and His totality. It is written with four letters. When the initial letter, *alif* is removed, the three remaining letters are the symbol of the universe, of existence, which consists of the visible world (*dunya*); and the invisible heavens above the starry firmament; purgatory (*barzakh*) and heaven; the hereafter (*akhira*). The first letter, *alif,* is the source of all, and the last letter, *hu* [He], is Allah's most perfect attribute free from all associations.)

people of this Way when they say that so-and-so is of Moses or Abraham or Enoch. Included among them is the trustee of two or three or four, or even more Words. The Perfected One is entrusted with the collectivity of Words, and he is of Muhammad particularly.

While he is at his destination, as long as he does not return, the seeker is called "one who stops" (*waqif*). Those who stop include the ones who are absorbed in that station, as for instance Abu-'Iqal and others. In it [God] takes them and in it they are resurrected.[30] The classification *waqif* also includes the ones who are sent back (*mardudun*). These are more perfect than the absorbed ones (*mustahlikun*), if they equal each other in station. If [one seeker] is absorbed in a higher station than that from which [another seeker] returns, then we do not say that the returned one is higher. The condition for drawing a comparison is the mutual resemblance of the two. If that condition is met, then the returned one lives, having descended from the station of the absorbed one, so that he reaches the degree of the absorbed one and surpasses him in drawing near, surpasses him in coming down, and excels him in development and reception of knowledge.

As for the returned ones, there are two types of men among them. There is one who returns to himself alone; he is the

inheritors of the prophets who first manifested them. The Prophet Muhammad, as the Seal or Completion of the prophets, holds within himself all of these prophetic Words.—*Trans.*

descender whom we have mentioned. This sort of man is the gnostic, *'arif*, among us. He returns to perfecting himself from other than the road which he traveled. Also among them is the one who is sent back to Creation with the language of direction and guidance. He is the inheriting knower, *'alim*.

Not all summoners to God and inheritors are in the same station, but the station of their calling gathers them together, and some of them surpass others in degree. As God Most High said, "We have made some of these messengers excel over others" [Koran 2:253]. Among the inheritors are summoners in the Word of Moses and Jesus and Shem and Noah and Isaac and Ishmael and Adam and Enoch and Abraham and Joseph and Aaron, and others; these are the Sufis. They are the adepts of states, in comparison to the masters among us.[31] Among [the inheritors] are also summoners in the Word of Muhammad (peace and blessing be upon him); these are the *Malamiyya,* the adepts of permanence and realities.

And when they summon Creation to God Most High, among them is the one who calls them from the door of *fana'* in the reality of servitude, (*'ubudiyya*).[32] [This *fana'* is referred to by] His saying (may He be exalted) "even as I created you before when you were nothing" [Koran 19:9]. And among them is the one who calls from the door of attention to servitude, which is lowliness and need and what the station of servitude requires. And among them is the one who calls from the door of attention to the Merciful nature; and the one who calls from the door of attention to the Vanquishing nature; and

Allah the Just, the one who knows the inner essence of things and the hidden. The one who is beneficent to His creation in the finest of ways. Allah the Clement.

the one who calls from the door of attention to the Divine nature, which is the fourth door and the most sublime of them.[33]

Know that prophethood and sainthood both share in three things: one, in knowledge without acquired learning; two, in action by *himma*, the heart's intention, in what is customarily believed not possible except through the body, or that for which the body has no capacity; three, in seeing the world of images in the sensory world. The two differ solely in their mode of addressing people, for the discourse of the saint is other than the discourse of the prophet.[34]

Do not suppose that the ascents of the saints equal the ascents of the prophets. This is not so, because ascents require particular undertakings. If saints and prophets shared in the same business by virtue of making the same ascent, then saints would be the same as prophets, and that is not the case with us.[35] Although the two classes share a common ground—the stations of divine realization—still the ascent of the prophets is through the fundamental light itself, while the ascent of the saints is through what is providentially granted by that light.[36] Though both [a saint and a prophet] might be in the station of Trust, for instance, it would not present the same aspect in both cases. Superiority is not found in the station of realization, but in its aspect. The aspects of trust depend upon the ones who trust, and the case is the same in every state and station of *fana'* and *baqa'*, union and separation, harmony and discord, and so forth.

And know that every saint of God Most High receives what he receives through the spiritual mediation of the prophet whose sacred Way he follows, and it is from that station that he contemplates. And there are those who know that, and those who do not know it and say, "God said to me"; but this is nothing other than the spiritual nature [of their prophet]. And there are secrets of His subtlety here for which these pages, intended only as an introduction, are too narrow.

Among the saints of the community of Muhammad—the Gatherer of the states of the prophets, peace and blessings be upon him—there may be an inheritor of the state of Moses, but he inherits from the Light of Muhammad, not from the Light of Moses. His state is from Muhammad, just as the state of Moses was from Muhammad. Sometimes a saint near his death will appear to pay heed to Moses or Jesus. Ordinary people and those without knowledge imagine that he has become a Jew or a Christian, since he mentions these prophets at the point of death, but [in fact this mention] stems from the power of the awareness which characterizes his station. The *qutb*, however, belongs directly to the heart of Muhammad. And we have encountered men belonging to the heart of Jesus—among them is the first shaykh whom you met—and men belonging to the heart of Moses, and others belonging to the heart of Abraham, and others [of similar attainment]. And this will remain a secret to all but our friends.

Know that Muhammad (peace and blessing be upon him) is he who gave all the prophets and messengers their stations in

Allah the Sustainer, the All-Knowing, the one whose orders and manifestations are wisdom, the Loving One and the only one worthy of love, the Powerful, Glorious, and Generous.

the World of Spirits until he was sent in the body.[37] We followed him [thus inheriting his direct guidance in the temporal world]. The prophets who witnessed him, or who descend after him,[38] join with us in this, and the saints of the prophets who preceded [his physical birth] receive [their spiritual inheritance] from Muhammad as well. So the saints of Muhammad share with the prophets in receiving [direct transmission] from him. Because of this it is reported in hadith: "The knowers of this community are like the prophets of Israel." And God Most High said concerning us, "... in order that you be witnesses of the people" [Koran 22:78]; and He said, concerning the Messengers, "And that day We will raise up from every community a witness against them from among themselves" [Koran 16:89]. So we and the prophets are the witnesses for their followers. Therefore devote *himma* in retreat to the entire legacy of Muhammad.

Know that the certain, enduring, perfect sage is he who treats every condition and moment in the appropriate manner, and does not confuse them. This is the state of Muhammad (peace and blessings be upon him) for he was two bow lengths' distance or less from his Lord; and when he awoke among his people and mentioned that to those who were present, the polytheists did not believe him, because no mark [of the ascension] appeared on him, and his appearance was the same as theirs. This was not possible even for Moses, who, when the mark [of Divine Revelation] appeared upon him, veiled himself.

JOURNEY TO THE LORD OF POWER

Every seeker inevitably will experience the impact of the states, and the blending of the worlds with one another, but the development from this stage to the stage of divine wisdom appearing within the customary outward principles is incumbent upon him. Transcendence of the customary order will become his secret, so that events beyond the ordinary will accompany him ordinarily. He will say unceasingly with every breath, "My Lord, increase me in knowledge while the heavenly sphere turns by Your breath,"[39] and let him strive that his Moment *be* His breath. When the influence of the Moment befalls him, he will receive it. Let him beware of becoming enamored of [the influence of the Moment] but let him remember it, for it will be necessary to him if he instructs. Most of the shaykhs are eliminated as teachers only by neglecting to remember what we have mentioned, and abstaining from it totally.

The Moment[40] lengthens and shortens in accordance with the presence of the one who partakes in it. There are those whose Moment is an hour or a day or a week or a month or a year or once in a lifetime. And [included] in humanity is the one who has no Moment. For the one who is heedful of the breaths has the hours in his power, and all that is beyond that; and the one whose Moment is the presence of the hours loses the breaths; and the one whose Moment is the days loses the hours; and the one whose Moment is the weeks loses the days; and the one whose Moment is the years loses the months; and the one whose Moment is his lifetime loses the years; and

He is the Creator, the Giver of shape and character, the Bestower of most beneficient gifts, the Pardoner of sins, the Overwhelming One.

whoever has no Moment has no lifetime and loses his afterlife. It does not prolong his animal *himma*. And personal elevation indicates the narrowness of one's Moment and the smallness of his knowledge.

The one who has no Moment is deprived of it only for the duration of his disease, for as long as he is ruled by his animal nature. For it is not possible for the door of the invisible world and its secrets to be opened while the heart craves for them.[41] As for the door of contemplative knowledge of God, it does not open so long as the heart glances toward anything in the world, visible or invisible.

And know concerning these matters entrusted [to us by God—the duties of Sacred Law]: If a person seeks them and carries them out, with no intention (*himma*) of any undertaking over and above them, except [hope for] Paradise—he is the worshipper, companion of water and the prayer niche. On the other hand, if someone's intention is connected to what is beyond worship without preparation for it, nothing will be revealed to him and his intention will not profit. On the contrary, such a person resembles one who is diseased. His strengths and capacities are completely nullified, and with him the will, *himma,* and ability to act become seriously damaged. How can he possibly reach what he seeks with his *himma?* Consequently preparation to perfection, with *himma* and more, is required.[42]

And if he reaches the essence of reality, and his intention is dissolved—and the attainment of what is beyond this has no limit—the attainer says: "It is not proper other than thus, and that only for the sake of the astonishment which occurs at the raising of the veils." For through the knowledge which arises in contemplation he turns to face what is beyond each appearance: the Truth beyond appearances. For the Apparent One, though He is one in essence, is infinite in aspects. They are His traces in us.[43]

And still the knower is thirsty continually forever, and desire and awe cleave to Him continually forever. And for the like of this let the workers work, and for the like of this let the contenders contend.

And may the blessings of God be upon our Master Muhammad, and upon his family and companions; and peace. And praise be to God, Lord of the Worlds.

Allah the One whose existence is endless.

NOTES
FROM THE COMMENTARY OF
'ABDUL-KARIM JILI

NOTES

1. *"a station less than the station of return."* Because absorption (*istihlak*) is a *fana'* in which one does not experience the multiplicity of the manifestations of the Essence or the variety of its descents into the Presence of the Names. This state of experience of multiplicity is one of the characteristics of *baqa'* after *fana'*, and is the cause of manifestation, the beloved knowledge for the sake of which He created the world.

2. *"knowledge of the matrices of realms."* In overview, not in detail. [The Realms] are not derivable until you know where you come from and where you are and where you are going. Then you will know in general what each one of them requires by its own essence or through reference to another Realm, or both. In this way you will be prepared to behave appropriately according to the Realm you are currently in, and according to the Realm to which you will be transported by your behavior here. And I will make clear what these Realms *"imply in this place"*—that is, in the Realm which you are in now, not what

they are absolutely. [Their absolute nature] you will encounter only when you are transported to them, so it is profitless to discuss it. The seeker must undertake what is most important; he must respect each Realm by giving it its proper due. For when a seeker is tranported from a Realm, if what he was required to attain there has escaped him, he will never accomplish it. This leads to his eternal failure. [According to the hadith] "one of the beauties of Islam is a man's leaving what does not concern him" and "Time is a cutting sword; if you do not cut it, it cuts you." [And as it is said] "The Sufi is the son of his moment"; and "The present does not return."

And know that the world vanishes into nonexistence in every moment by the overwhelming victory of the Unity (*ahadiyya*) over the multiplcity. And its like is produced [at every moment] by the authority of essential love. For the world's existence is the instant of its nonexistence. Thus the Manifest imposes manifestation upon the first hiddenness, and the world is produced. Next the Hidden imposes hiddenness upon the first manifestation, and the world vanishes. Then the authority returns to the Manifest—and so forth, ad infinitum. This is what is termed "renewed creation" (*khalq jadid*). The imaginary prolongation which seems to result from this flowing of similitudes is Time; and motion is its measure.

Everything that is other than God is temporal. And if it is impossible that the [real] duration of an event exceed an instant, then *every* happening is "the son of its moment," and not other than it. The event is necessary to its moment, and the moment is necessary to its event. Rather, the moment essentially determines its event, which cannot be separated out of it. Thus the moment is the event's locus, or realm (*watan*). The moments are infinite; therefore the realms are also infinite.

And know that the renewal of similitudes [which is imagined as Time] proceeds so that a thing vanishes and its like follows it—White becomes nonexistent, and White is produced. If it were to vanish and its opposite follow it—if White is made to vanish and Black is produced—that would alter the nature of things.

And if the loci of the similitudes are their moments, the loci of the moments would be the forms from which the similitudes are renewed. The Universal Realms, in relation to the totality of the realms, resemble the matrix composed of these forms, and for this reason the shaykh said, *"The Realms is a term for the substrata of the moments in which things come to exist and experience actually occurs;"* that is to say, by proceeding from nonexistence to existence by renewed creation. This substratum is where the happening is while it happens. So understand, for it is a delicate point.

"It is necessary," O student, after your knowledge of the Realms, *"that you know what the Truth wants from you in any Realm"* in which you are present *"so that you hasten to it"* and produce it in the best fashion *"without hesitation"* that is, without engagement in a matter that hinders you from it, for that leads to your destruction, *"and without resistance"* which

you find in yourself owing to the difficulty of what God asks of you—for that leads to your laziness and failure to produce it immediately.

3. *"The Realms"* about which we have promised to inform you, *"although many"* from the point of view of their particularity and their enumeration's surpassing human capacity, *"are all derived"* comprehensively *"from six."*

"The first Realm" is the Realm of *"Am I not your Lord?"* This is the Realm where you were before your physical existence, in the form of an atom among a crowd of spirits. And you knew what God wished of you in this Realm when He caused you to know that He had designated your singularity out of sheer generosity and kindness. So you hastened to accomplish [what was desired of you there] immediately, without hesitating, because He willed it and demanded it directly. The authority of His Will is irresistible, especially when demand is simultaneous with it through removal of intermediaries.

That which he asked of you in that Realm was affirmation of His Lordship. He said (may He be exalted) "And when your Lord took the sons of Adam from their manifestation as atoms and called them to witness against themselves: 'Am I not your Lord?' They answered: Yes" [Koran 7:172]. And here is a subtle secret known by one who is familiar with the reality of duty and responsibility.

Then when you descended from the pinnacle of the world

of spirits to the depths of the world of bodies, you forgot that Realm and what happened to you in it. And if you turn to God searchingly, you will remember, God willing, [your affirmation of his Lordship]. And you will say, in that event, what the Seal of the Saints of Muhammad [Shaykh Ibn 'Arabi], may God be pleased with him, said in verse:

> I bore witness to you as King before our existence
> Through what the eye saw in a handful of atoms,
> A particular witness whose being I now understand.
> At the time of testimony there was no deception,
> The road I took was plainly and joyfully taken.
> I was not a prisoner in the grip of confinement.

The shaykh has referred to the separation from this Realm by his comment *"our physical existence has removed us from this Realm."*

"The world we are now in" [The second Realm], according to the shaykh, runs from the concave surface of the Sphere of Heavenly Mansions to the surface of the earth.

"The Interval" (*al-barzakh;* the third Realm) is the barrier between this world and the next. The shaykh (may God be pleased with him) said:

> Know that "interval" is an expression for something which separates two other things, like the dividing line between sun and shade, and as He said—may He be

73

exalted—concerning the mixture of the two seas, "Between them is a barrier (*barzakh*) which they cannot cross" [Koran 55:20]. The meaning of "they cannot cross" is that they cannot mix with one another because of this partition which divides them. The sense of sight does not discern it. When suddenly it is perceived, the barrier does not exist. And when the barrier is between the known and the unknown, the nonexistent and the existent, the negated and the affirmed, and the rational and the irrational, it is called Interval—and [this Interval] is the imagination.

For if you perceive it—and you are rational—you know that your vision has encountered an existent thing, while you know unequivocally that it is not a "thing" completely and fundamentally. And what is this whose "thingness" is affirmed and denied simultaneously? The imagination is not existent or nonexistent, not known or unknown, not negated and not affirmed. And the human being travels to this reality in his sleep and after his death, and he sees descriptive qualities as existing embodied forms, and there is no doubt of that. And the intuitive person sees in his waking state what the sleeper sees in the state of sleep and the deceased sees after death.

"The fourth Realm is the Resurrection" and it is the gathering of men *"on the awakening earth"* [see Koran 79:14]. It is the

surface of the earth, and is called "awakening" because in it
are their wakefulness and sleep. The shaykh said:

Know, O brother, when the people stand in their
graves and God Most High wills that the earth become
other than the earth, that the earth will stretch by the
permission of God and a bridge will be made over the
darkness. The whole creation will be upon it. Then God
will transform the earth as He wills, how He wills, into
another earth called "awake"; and it is an earth in the
knowledge of God: Nothing sleeps upon it. God
Glorious and Exalted will stretch it like a skin. In the
expansion of it that He wills He will strengthen the
weakness of what it was [by stretching it out] from
twenty-one parts to ninety-nine: He will stretch it like a
skin. You will not see in it crookedness or deviation.

"and the return to the original condition." This original
condition" (*hafira*) by its etymological origins means the way
in which a man came. It is said "so-and-so returned in his
original condition" when he returned as he came. And the
meaning of the saying "I am of those who return in the original
condition" is that we return living after death.

"The fifth Realm is the Garden," and it is between the
concavity of the starless sphere and the convexity of the
Sphere of Heavenly Mansions, and *"the Fire,"* which is from
the concavity of the Sphere of Heavenly Mansions to the

center of the earth. For the seven heavens and the elements will change their form, after the division and judgment, into Hell.

"The sixth Realm is the Sand Dune" [See Koran 73:14]. It is a hill of white musk where the creatures are at the time of the vision of God Glorious and Exalted. It is *"outside the Garden"* because it is in the Garden of Eden which is the stronghold and citadel outside the other Gardens. The majority of people will not enter the Presence and Qualities of the King except by virtue of visiting this place.

"In each of these" six Realms to which we have alluded *"are places which are Realms within Realms, and the realization of them in their multiplicity is not within human power. In our situation we need only an explanation of the Realm of this world, which is the place of responsibility, trial"* that is, testing, *"and works,"* which necessitate [Divine] blessing in the Realms which follow. For there is no Realm among the Realms which is the site of obligation [specifically, the obligation to choose God's service, (*taklif*)] except this one. This fact points to the secret of [the saying] "The moment does not extend its reward."

And if you were to say that the moral responsibility of children and madmen will certainly arrive in the Realm of the Resurrection, and that our present world is the root of the remainder of Realms, so that the Realms of the Interval, the Resurrection, the Garden and Fire, and the Sand Dune are degrees belonging to the manifestation of this worldly Realm, you might consequently hold that all these Realms depend specifically on obligation. Understand that this is not the case. For if you consider it, you will find that obligation is a [constituting] reality of the Realm of the present world. However, if it appears in the Resurrection, it does not appear there because it is essential that it do so. The Resurrection, unlike the Realm of the present world, does not fundamentally require obligation. It requires reckoning and apportionment— nothing else. Similarly, if [the present world] requires obligation by its essential structure, it might also require apportionment through something other than its essential structure, just as the Resurrection acquires obligation through something other than its essence.

And the shaykh does not allude [further] to the matrices of Realms, but states that we have no need to describe any of them here except for the Realm of the present world.

4. *"absorption in the Real by means of obliteration from the worlds."* This is a technical turn of phrase. The shaykh said that "obliteration" (*mahq*) is your appearing in existence in the world, through Him, in vice-regency and deputyship from Him, so that the dominion of the world belongs to you. And "obliteration of obliteration" (*mahq al-mahq*) is your appearing in His veil. In "obliteration of obliteration" you veil Him, so people encounter you as a creation without right [of rule]. For they cannot know that God sent you as a veil before them until they turn their eyes to Him. Thus "obliteration of obliteration" stands in contrast to "obliteration"; it is not an

exaggerated development of obliteration. Rather, it is like "the nonexistence of nonexistence."

Indeed the servant at his departure from the presence of God to the Creation is endowed with the means of acting as a ruler among the people. Of this they are not conscious, although they may have heard of some of these rulers as Messengers (the peace and blessings of God be upon them) whom God once sent as his vice-regents on earth in order to impart His judgment. God has concealed this capacity in the inheritors [of the prophets], who are nonetheless vice-regents even when there is no awareness of them.

And know that among the people of God "obliteration of obliteration" is completed in this world, and "obliteration" is completed in the next. And only the most elect of the people of God succeed with the obliteration of obliteration; it is for the illuminated intellects. The elect succeed with obliteration; it is for the illuminated souls. May God make us part of the obliteration of His obliteration, and may His right be attributed to Him alone.

5. *"the masters among us are scornful of this."* We are not advocating contemplation and *fana'* and absorption in the Real by obliteration in this world. Indeed *"the masters among us"*—companies of saints—*"are scornful of this."* Pertaining to this is His saying, may He be exalted: "The Messiah by no means disdained that he is a servant of God" [Koran 4:172]. *"Because it is a waste of time"* which we ought not to spend except in

NOTES

struggle, observation, and the acquisition of the divine sciences of piety; and because it means *"a loss of [true] rank"* in vision and obliteration in the next world.

For the vision of God in the next world corresponds to the measure of the knowledge of God acquired here. Therefore, this world is for the acquisition of knowledge with effort. The next is the abode of ease and contemplation. In the time you spend in contemplation in this world you lose a knowledge which, had you acquired it, would have increased your contemplation in the next. Thus contemplation in this world, which brings about your lack of acquisition of this knowledge, is a loss of contemplative rank to you in the next world, for contemplation corresponds to the measure of knowledge. You contemplated Him in *this* world only after knowing Him to some extent, and you beheld only the form of your knowledge. That knowledge which formed the basis of your contemplation was acquired in the pursuit of a greater knowledge. Had you attained the greater knowledge, your contemplation would have correspondingly deepened. If contemplation escapes you in this world on account of the pursuit of knowledge, it will not escape you in the next; but if knowledge escapes you in this world on account of contemplation—for it is a *fana'* with which there is no consciousness—contemplation will escape you in the next. This is loss of visionary rank.

As for its loss in regard to obliteration: Know that manifestation of deputyship and vice-regency is not suitable except in the next world, where there is neither obligation nor petrification of categories of being. In the next world [duplicating the Koranic description of the creative action of God], *man* says to a thing "Be," and it is. Thus it was reported that God sends to the people of the Garden a message with the following contents (and God knows best): "A letter from the Life Everlasting to the Life Everlasting. I say to a thing 'Be,' and it is, and I have made you to say to a thing 'Be,' and it is,"—and they do not say to a thing "Be" except that it is. This is the essence of the manifestation of vice-regency, and the world is not suitable for that. For this world is the house of work and responsibility, and the degree to which vice-regency appears here, is the degree to which it is lost in the next world. As God Most High has said, "You used up your blessings in the life of this world" [Koran 46:20].

However, this is the case only when the manifestation of the vice-regency in this world is not from the Divine Order. When it is from the Divine Order—as it was for the Messengers—they do not scorn it for what it contains of what *"associates the Realm"*—which is this world—*"with that which is unsuitable to it"*: the manifestation of vice-regency and the abandonment of the acquisition of knowledge.

6. "*khalwa.*" The shaykh said: "Know—and may God Most High grant us success—that the root of *khalwa* is in the Sacred Law: 'Whoever remembers Me in himself I remember him in Myself, and whoever remembers Me in assembly, I remember him in an assembly better than his' [*hadith qudsi*]." The root of

NOTES

khalwa is *al-khala'*, the void in which the world existed [before its creation].

7. *"It is better if your food be nourishing"* so that the constitution will not become imbalanced with a predominance of dryness, *"but devoid of animal fat"* because animal fat strengthens animality, and its principles will dominate the spiritual principles.

8. *"If there should be an influence which alters the constitution,"* like the pains which used to seize the Messenger of God from the advent of Gabriel upon him and [the Koran's] descent upon his pure heart. This state was expressive of [Gabriel's] presence. Because [angelic nature] is not compatible with [man's nature], it used to be very difficult for the Prophet; his constitution was strained, and his brow would perspire.

9. *"you will not undergo any alteration in form."* If the influx were to originate at the level of abstract essences and arrive upon you at the level of the world of images, then you would suffer no alteration in form through its influence in you.

10. *"until God drives the demonic influences from it [your heart]."* For God is the companion of the one who mentions Him, and the devil is distant from God Most High; so God and the devil are never found in the same company.

11. *"If you are offered something to drink"* in this unveiling, *"choose water,"* for it is the form of absolute knowledge. *"If there is no water among the offerings, choose milk,"* the symbol of pure original religion, as the Messenger, peace and blessings be upon him, did when he ascended to Heaven [and was presented with a similar choice]. For milk is the form of knowledge of the sacred Ways. *"And if both of them are presented to you, combine the water and the milk"* because that is the form of the relationship between the remainder of knowledges and the ordained sacred legal knowledge, that is, the relation of each one of them to it and its relation to each of them. *"This also applies to honey: Drink it,"* for it is the form of the permissible philosophical knowledge and the sanctified systems laid down by philosophers and deviated priesthoods for the purpose of pleasing God. *"Be careful of drinking wine"* unmixed. You will be led astray by it—for it is the form of the knowledge of states—*"unless it is mixed with rainwater,"* which is the form of knowledge granted [by God], by which you will be rightly guided. The states, when devoid of divinely granted knowledges which contain no error, mislead those that partake of them. *"Even if it is mixed with the water of rivers and springs,"* which is the form of natural knowledge, *"refrain from drinking it"* because it leads to heresy and apostasy and the corruption of opinions. And if it were mixed with well-water, which is the form of intellectual knowledge, it is the same. For when the states are muddled by thought, error increases and correctness diminishes. Drink the water of rivers and springs

unmixed, and also when mixed with rainwater or milk, but do not drink it when mixed with well-water or honey. And do not drink well-water unless it is mixed with rainwater or milk.

12. *"This ascent is the ascent of dissolution"* because material origins dissolve in it, as the shaykh has indicated. And their disintegration is only in relation to the consciousness of the seeker, as their arrangement was only by relation to his consciousness. You certainly will know the reality of that. This dissolution is only of *"the order"* among the elements in the exterior world.

...You know that *"the state of contraction* (qabd) *will accompany you"* in your discovery and examination of all of *"these worlds"* because you are in the ascent of dissolution in which your essence vanishes; and that requires contraction, without a doubt.

13. *"the infusion of the world of life force"*...like the life that appeared through the hand of Jesus, upon whom be peace, in those living creatures that were vivified because of him, as for instance the human dead whom he raised and the birds of clay which he brought to life. The effect this life-force had in every dead creature which he brought to life by it corresponded to the pre-existent structure of that being. For instance, if the essence were the essence of a bird, a bird came to life, and if the essence were the essence of a man, a man came to life, the life-force remaining a single reality [independent of the bird,

the man, and any other revivified form]. Its effects differ in accordance with the varieties of pre-existent structure exposed to it.

"And how the expressions [of faith] are included in this infusion," as, for instance, His saying (may He be exalted) "when you shaped from clay the likeness of a bird by My permission, and blew upon it and it was a bird, by My permission, and you healed him who was born blind and the leper by My permission, and when you raised the dead by My permission" [Koran 5:110], and His saying "I breathe into it and it becomes a bird, by Allah's leave, I heal him born blind and the leper and I raise the dead, by Allah's leave" [Koran 3:49].

14. *"surface signs."* I do not know the meaning of the "surface signs" (*al-lawa'ih al-lawhiyya*), but we have knowledge of the "signs of state."

. . . Know that the shaykh, may God be pleased with him, said: " 'The signs' (*lawa'ih*), to the People of God, means the elevation from state to state that begins to appear to their inner sensitivity. To us, it means the essential lights—the transcendent glory seen from the perspective of affirmation rather than of negation—and the lights of the Divine Names which appear at the contemplation of their effects. All this becomes visible to the eye unrestricted by greed." So you will distinguish these lights.

As for the elevation from state to state, it is that one does not return to a state after having left it for something higher.

The object [of a state] is the divine influences and knowledges of God which it brings. [The states themselves] are stages, not gifts of special grace. They may return repeatedly, but the one experiencing them does not offer praise for them except when they increase his knowledge of God, [which is not necessarily the case].

15. *"the light of the ascendant stars."* The shaykh said: " 'The ascendant stars' (*tawali'*) is a technical expression used to mean the lights of the declaration of unity (*tawhid*) arising in the hearts of the gnostics, which extinguish the rest of the lights"—meaning the lights of speculative proofs, not those of prophetic, revelatory proofs. And they extinguish as well the lights of intuition. This is the *tawhid* desired by God from His worshipper. The part of speculative thought in it is only the declaration of unity of degree; His existence as the object of worship particularly, so that there is nothing that can be worshipped other than He. Concerning this, he says, the evidence is clear.

16. *"the form of the universal order."* This is an expression for the appearance of God in the form of Creation. And you will know that the essential existence is composed of *haqq*, Truth, and *khalq,* Creation; but you will not attain this until you pass beyond the light of the ascendant stars.

17. *"the degrees of speculative sciences"* corresponding to

actuality. You will know which of them are higher and which of them are lower and which should precede and which should follow. And He reveals to you the reality of *"sound integral ideas"* straight and free from error *"and the forms of perplexing questions which confuse understanding"* so that the constitutions of those who consider them become unbalanced, *"and the difference between supposition and knowledge"*—and there are few among the people of knowledge who know this. Most observers make no difference between them in most cases. And *"the birth of possibilities between the world of spirits and the physical world"* as Jesus was brought to birth between Mary and Gabriel, peace be upon them, and the soul between the spirit and the body; and the cause of this conception.

18. *"the infusion of the Divine Mystery in the domain of His loving concern."* This is the unity of the Essence in the world of the Names, the unity of the Intellect in the world of spirits, and the unity of the Throne in the world of bodies. This unity is the essence of mercy. The unity penetrates into the people of God's concern until it pervades their essences, their attributes, and their actions as it pervades the Divine Essence, Intellect, and Throne, and that character appears in the king and the ant among them. With the people of misfortune the opposite applies.

But if you can climb with me and follow me, say: There is no misfortune. For the Divine Mystery pervades the entirety of the world, and there is no misfortune. All of what God has arranged is the domain of His loving concern, because it is in the grasp of the Real. What is in His grasp is near Him, and what is near God is good and preserved; misfortune is evil and there is no evil in Him. So understand! I have approached by steps in these words a sea of realities and knowledges. If you attain the depth of it and bring out its pearls, then you are the master of your moment. And God, may He be exalted, is the Guide. There is no Lord other than Him.

19. *"And there is nothing that pertains to a station,"* to any state or station previously mentioned, *"which He reveals to you"* among the heavens, the elements, and the living creatures *"that does not greet you with honor, reverence, and exaltation; its degree of the Divine Presence is made clear to you, and [each one] loves you in its essence."* This is a test of God Most High, so that He knows the soundness of your concentration on Him and the sincerity of your search for Him and your turning away from what is other than He. If you become enamored of the precious things that He unfolds before you and stop with them, you will be driven from His door and lost. And if you persevere in His quest and turn away from other than Him and arrive in His Holy Presence, you triumph and are victorious and gain command, by His order, over all that had been spread before you.

20. *"the world of bewilderment."* He made it a world of *"bewilderment and helplessness and inability"* because the light of

the inexpressible being-nature of God (*huwiyya*) encompasses it, and no one can see it or perceive it through the intensity of its light. And gazing upon the being-nature bequeaths life, as cannot be denied.

21. *"and you sway like a lamp"* in the blowing of the breeze. Know (may God have mercy upon you) that this place is a stage demanding the greatest courage from seekers. For if they arrive in it and this oneness manifests itself to them, and this light which the shaykh has mentioned rises upon them, they suppose that they have arrived in the Presence of the Unity (*ahadiyya*) and triumphed in the essential revelation. This occurs because of the Divine bliss they find in this stage and the fact that any reality other than their own is absent from it. So, O Seeker on these paths, if you arrive at this revelation, do not be bound by it, and do not desire it for its bliss and delight.

22. *"And veils are lifted. And veils descend"* upon *"the forms of the sons of Adam."* And this is because when the first of us [Adam] disobeyed God Most High, his form altered. A veil from the Name *al-Sattar,* the Veiler, descended between [Adam's altered form] and the rest of the forms so that they did not know what had befallen the man, or the alteration with which his transgression had marked him. When he repented, his form returned to what it had been. So the veil was lifted from Adam and the rest of the forms saw him in his original state. This issues from the mercy and generosity of God. . . .

NOTES

23. *"a special praise which upon hearing you recognize."* And it is: "Exalted is He Who reveals the beautiful and conceals the ugly."

24. *"And if you do not stop with this,"* that is, with the Throne of the Merciful, *"He reveals to you. . . the First Intellect"* which is the first teacher, and the first existence of the world of record and inscription. It is the director and emanator of everything by permission and order of God Most High. Hence it is *"the master of everything"*, "everything" meaning the Throne, the Soul of the Universe. For the Intellect transmits to the Soul all that is received from God Most High. When the Throne is called a Tablet, the Intellect is the Pen (*al-qalam*) which writes upon it; when it is called a Soul, the Intellect is its Master. Thus the Intellect is its *"teacher."* *"You examine its tracing"* in the realities of the world and the reality of its state, and know *"the message it bears. . . . And witness its inversion"* insofar as it is a Pen, for the sake of writing on the Tablet. For, when you write with a Pen, it is inverted. And you witness *"its reception"* of the comprehensive knowledge [as in filling a pen with ink], and the *"particularization of the comprehensive [knowledge]"* in the Tablet *"from the angel* al-Nuni." In regard to learning His language, they are like the governing and governed elements of a genitive construction.

Know that the shaykh wrote in his book *'Uqlat al-mustawfiz* ("The Spell of the Obedient Servant") that there is no mediator between the Intellect and the Creator, Glory to Him, although it is said that between Him and it is an angel called *al-Nuni* ["like the letter *nun*," the Abbreviated Letter which opens the Seventieth Sura of the Koran, called the Pen], which comprises the universal knowledge and is like an inkwell, the Intellect like a pen, and the Soul like a tablet. This is not correct. Rather the Intellect in regard to the comprehensiveness of knowledge in its essence is called *al-Nuni;* and activating the details of this knowledge by writing them on the Tablet is called the Pen.

25. *"And if you do not stop with this,"* that is, with the Master of everything which is the Highest Pen, *"He reveals the Mover"* of this Pen. It is *"the right hand of the Truth,"* meaning His attributes of Beauty, for they are what is required for the existence of the world. This is why they activate the Pen. So understand; if God wills, you shall be rightly guided.

And if you do not stop with this He reveals to you the Enraptured Angels created from the Cloud. And if you do not stop with them, He reveals to you the Cloud in which our Lord existed before He created the world* and the Word, the message of the Sublime to us, opened us into His reality. The shaykh, may God Most High be pleased with him, said:

The Cloud is the seat of the name "the Lord" (*al-*

---

*The Prophet was asked: "Where was your Lord before the creation of the world?" He replied: "In a cloud. There was no space either above or below." —*Trans.*

Rabb) as the Throne is the seat of the name "the Merciful" (*al-Rahman*). The Cloud is the first of things. Within it appeared the conditions of space and degree in Him Who does not enter into place or degree. From it manifested the substrata [of all possible existences], so that it receives the abstract essences of embodiment (*al-ma'ani al-jismaniyya*) of the sensory and imaginal worlds. It is an exalted existent whose abstract essence is the Truth; it is the truth by which everything is created, and not other than God Most High. It is the entity in which the source-forms of all beings are fixed and abide. It receives the reality of possibilities and the condition of place and the rank of degree, and the name "the Site." And from the earth to this Cloud there are no Names of God Most High except Names of actions. In the whole world, intelligible and perceivable, between these two extremes, there is no trace of anything other than this in existence.

And know that if you do not stop with the Cloud, He reveals to you the Breath of the Merciful (*al-nafas al-rahmani*). It is the source of the Cloud.

And if you do not stop with this, He reveals to you the side of the Names of Transcendence. Then Names of actions depart. You will learn the knowledge of negation, and be honored above the whole of the world. And you will know the degree necessary to you.

26. *"And if you do not stop with this"* you are raised to the essential oneness and *"eradicated"* there. The shaykh said:

> Eradication (*mahw*) to the elect, may God be pleased with them, is eradication of habitual characteristics and the removal of defect, and of what the Real veils and negates. He—may He be exalted—said, "God eradicates and establishes what He wills" [Koran 13:39]. Consequently He established eradication. Among the legalists, this is expressed as "abrogation." It is a divine abrogation. God Most High raises [whom He chooses] and eradicates him after he has had a determination in positive existence and being. This, both in things and in their principles, means the termination of the interval allotted to their existence, and crossing the boundary which continues to "an appointed time" [Koran 6:2]. For He said, "Everything continues to an appointed time and is established until a designated moment" [Koran 20:129]. Then He eliminates its determination, not its essential form (*'ayn*), for He said "continuing to an appointed *time"* [and the essential forms do not exist in time]. And when the appointed time arrives his "continuation" (or "flow") ceases, but his original form remains.

27. *"then withdrawn."* The Shaykh said:

NOTES

Absence (*ghayba*), to the people, is the heart's absence from knowledge of what passes in the world, through its being occupied with what impresses it. When it is merely this, it is only absence from a divine manifestation. It is not correct that absence be through some created thing that moves one; [rather it should be] because one is [truly] occupied, absent from the conditions of the world. And by this the Group [of the people of Truth] is distinguished from others, because absence [per se] exists virtually in all groups. The absence of this party is with truth, from creation, so in relation to them [absence] is noble and praiseworthy.

And the people of God Most High have degrees of absence, although they are all absences in truth. The absence of the gnostics is absence with truth from truth; the absence of the rest of the people of God Most High is absence with truth from Creation. The absence of the greatest of the knowers of God is an absence with Creation from Creation, because they have realized that there is no existence except God, Who shapes the possible determinations of the unchanging original forms.

28. *"then crushed."* This is an expression for the disappearance of the structure of your reality through the dominating power of the disclosure of the Essential Oneness.

29. *"you are affirmed."* The shaykh, may God be pleased with
him, said:

Affirmation [or fixity; *ithbat*] is the predestined order of
the whole world. So whoever seeks the repeal of the
habitual order certainly violates *adab,* the rule of right
conduct, and is ignorant. What some people call the
disruption of habit is itself a habit, since the constant
disruption of habit is a habit.

So custom is not obliterated except in its affirmation.
But [for this to be the case] the one who undertakes this
affirmation must be connected to the Real, and it must
be for the sake of this connection that he establishes the
customary principles. For his Friend has laid them
down, out of friendship and accord. How can one be
His friend and connected to Him while deciding against
Him in the elimination of what Wisdom has seen fit to
affirm? Especially since the partaker in this station
certainly knows that God is "a Wise and Knowing
One" in what He establishes and causes to be. So he will
affirm what his Friend affirms. If he does not do this,
and instead seeks the obliteration [of what God has
affirmed], he is a disputer. Whoever disputes with you
is not your friend, and you are not his friend. Such a one
is close to intransigence. But the friend of affirmation is
perpetually in connection with the Truth, so that he
affirms the customary principles and witnesses Him in

them. One is not firmly established in this [friendship]
if he seeks [even the momentary] repeal of laws and not
their obliteration.

30. *"While"* the attainer is held fast *"at his destination"* where
his seeking ended, *"he is called 'one who stops'* (al-waqif)"—the
seized, the consumed; and to him is attributed half of
perfection, "going with no coming," *"as long as he does not
return."* When he returns, the perfection of perfection is
attributed to him. *"Those who stop"* means those who attain the
destinations of the roads assigned by their predispositions. For
there are no ends except in relation to beginnings. The
existence of an absolute finality is unimaginable; otherwise the
realities would be overthrown.

"The ones who are absorbed in that station," which is the end of
their road, *"as for instance Abu-'Iqal"* al-Maghribi, among the
great Attainers, *"and others"* like Abu-Yazid Bistami, who,
when he arrived among the seekers of the Presence, was
honored with the robe of vice-regency and deputyship and was
told, "Go out to My creation in My form, and whoever sees
you, sees Me...." *"In it"* meaning in that station in which
they are absorbed, *"[God] takes them and in it they are
resurrected"* because a person dies as he lived, and is resurrected
as he died.

31. *"They are adepts of states, in comparison to the masters among
us,"* who are adepts of stations.

95

32. " *'ubudiyya.*" Know that *'ubudiyya,* servitude, is the essential characteristic of the servant. It is the essence of poverty, meaning possibility. *'Ubudiyya* is undivided attention to the contemplation proper to a servant, its continuous observance in every state, station, revelation, disclosure, contemplation, and stage. And service is what proceeds in accordance with the requirements of servanthood. *Fana'* in *'ubudiyya* means the nonexistence of contemplation [from the position of] lordship, and equal concentration upon whatever aspect [of the Real presents itself].

33. *"the most sublime of them"*—because it encompasses [all] the doors...and summons [the people] to the totality of Names.

34. *"The two differ solely in their mode of addressing people, for the discourse of the saint is other than the discourse of the prophet."* The saint addresses whoever is behind and following him. The prophet addresses whoever is before him, through fundamental authority, not through their following. And the saint speaks from behind the veil of his prophet, while the prophet speaks without a veil—that is, without the mediation of another prophet.

35. *"that is not the case with us"* because the follower, insofar as he is a follower, never attains the station of the one he follows at all. And he is not a saint except insofar as he is a follower, for his sainthood is the essence of his following.

36. *"the ascent of the prophets is by the fundamental light,"* that is, the divinely revealed knowledge. "Fundamental" because it pours forth to them from the origin, not subsequently, and they are not prophets except through their rising by this light. *"While the ascent of the saints is through what is providentially granted"* to a predisposition for sainthood *"by that light,"* which falls upon whoever stands in it. A level of sainthood possesses the fundamental light only in the extent apportioned to its original form. The predisposition for sainthood is nothing else.

The capacity of the saints accrues through human effort. So the saint ascends only on the strength of that fundamental light which befalls him in proportion to what he has earned. This rising is by the light, because the ascent of the Truth is dark to the eyes of the gnostics. This light is the revealed knowledge with which He enlightens them. It is given to the prophets without preparation. On account of this, prophethood cannot be earned. This is a true saying and the opinion of the shaykh. And it is given to the saints only by means of their earned capacity through works which they have received from the prophets. The works of the mind have no part in this preparation, for sainthood is earned through the works of Sacred Law, not those of thinking.

37. *"Know that Muhammad"* through [as stated in the famous hadith] his being a prophet while Adam was between water and clay, *"is he who gave all the prophets and messengers"* their

sciences, sacred Ways, and *"stations"* and states *"in the World of Spirits,"* because he is the guardian of the divine secrets. For his spirit is the First Intellect, treasurer of the Divine and principle of the world of record and inscription, the reality of the first determination which is the origin of all determinations. So according to the Name "the Hidden," by his reality and spirit he is giver of all that is given. According to the Name "the Manifest," all who give gifts are his deputies and followers. They receive from him in the Name of the Hidden, and dictate to the world in the Name of the Manifest. And thus their rule did not cease *"until he was sent in the body,"* the physical body, to "the black and the red" [races; that is, all of mankind].

38. *"...the prophets who witnessed him"* at the time of his appearance in the body, like Khidr, peace be upon him, who according to the shaykh is one of the prophets, and who met with, received from, and followed the Messenger in the material world. This expression does not refer to anything which sacred tradition contradicts [i.e., one is not to understand it as disputing the dignity of Muhammad as the last of the prophets], because that is not correct either by transmitted teaching or by intuition.

"or who descend" from heaven *"after him,"* that is, after Muhammad. This is Jesus, peace be upon him, who will descend at the end of time, rule by our Law, kill swine, break crosses, and call men to the community of Muhammad, peace

and blessings be upon him. He is the Seal of the General
Sainthood.

39. *"events beyond the ordinary will accompany him ordinarily."*
[He will possess] full consciousness in relation to all states as
they come into existence. This is necessary for the "accurate
balance of the scales" [Koran 55:9] and the nonexistence of
"short weight and measure."

"He will say unceasingly with every breath..." of the breaths
the Merciful, whose object is renewed creation; or by another
reading, with every human breath—and this is the more
obvious interpretation.

"while the heavenly sphere turns by His breath." The shaykh
said: "Then you will know the Sufi saying that the heavenly
sphere revolves through the breaths of the world, meaning the
world that is breathed. That is, the cause of its revolution is the
existence of the breaths; with its revolution, God renews the
breaths."

40. *"The Moment"* (*waqt*) is an expression for your state in
time. The state does not attach itself to the past or the future.
It is an existent between two nonexistents. And if your
Moment is the wellspring of your state, you are the son of your
Moment, and your Moment determines what you are, because
it is existent and you are nonexistent, you are illusory and it is
affirmed. If your Moment is obedience, and the contemplation
proper to servitude in every state, then you are one of the

enduring. And if it is the opposite of that, then you are one of the ephemeral. In the first case your Moment is closeness, and in the second case it is distance: In any case, the Moment will inevitably give you its experience. If your Moment is closeness, your experience is from the Presence of closeness; and if your moment is distance, your experience is from the Presence of distance. And whoever mourns over the past and fills the present moment with the past, he is one of those made distant. For he lets slip by what the current state demands, engrossed in what will not return. This is the essence of nonexistence. And whoever occupies himself with the future is in the same state.

41. *"while the heart craves from them"* because craving (*shahwa*), as the shaykh said, is a limited natural desire. Consequently craving does not attach itself to any object except by the inclination of a natural drive. If someone discovers in himself an inclination to something without the involvement of a natural drive—as for instance his inclination to abstract meanings and high spiritual essences and perfection and the vision and knowledge of God—then he need not withdraw from this inclination. But if he is inclined to these things through the pleasure of deceptive imaginings, then that [same inclination] is the attachment of craving. [It is attraction] on account of the form. For the imagination, when it has made corporeal that which has no form—and this stems from the action of nature—simply stops.

100

NOTES

...The Shaykh said: "Will is a divine spiritual natural attribute.... If inclination connects to the immaterial without imagination...It is an inclination of will, not of natural desire. For craving has no entry to entities independent of matter, but will has connection to every object of the soul and intellect, whether that object be attractive [to the appetites] or not. Craving has no connection except to the soul's obtaining a particular pleasure."

42. "himma *and more*"—external worship, which is the perfection of his exterior.

43. *"And if"* the seeker is adorned with the preparation we have described, and *"he reaches the essence of reality"*—and that is the essence of realization in form—*"and his intention is dissolved"*—that is to say, his will in the Will of God—he knows that his will is a branch of the will of God. God Most High has said, "And you do not will other than what God wills" [Koran 76:30]. If God had not willed the seeker to reach Him, he would not have done so. There are more passages concerning this in the Koran than can be counted, and among them is His saying "He turned to them so that they would turn to Him" [Koran 9:118]; and "He loves them so they love Him" [Koran 5:54]. For reality is the negation of the vestiges of your attributes by His attributes, since He is the agent through you, in you, from you, and you are not. "And there is no living creature except that He seizes it by the forelock"

[11:56]. The dissolution of *himma* is the essence of the realization of the human being in form [that is, in his true essential human form], because his attributes at that time are the essence of the attributes of God. So understand.

And know that the journey to God is limited, because it means the crossing of the illusory distance [between man and God] which is the essence of the world. And as for the journey *in* God, and that is the knowledge of Him in His attributes, it is infinite; because His attributes (may He be exalted) are without end. Therefore the attainment to God has an end, *"and the attainment of what is beyond this has no limit."*

The one who has arrived says in the voice of *"the attainer"*— the one in whom some of the aspects of God, His Names, have arisen— *"It is not proper"* that God exist within the limitation of his essence *"other than thus"*—than what the attainer has become. For [in any other case] it would limit Him, and He, Glory to Him, is unconditioned and without boundary. Or according to another understanding of this sentence: "It is not necessary" that what has occurred should have happened as it did—and this is more obvious—but it happened *"for the sake of the astonishment which occurs at the raising of the veils."* And all things are the faces of God, which are His essential form. And *"through the knowledge which arises in contemplation he turns to face what is beyond each appearance,"* that is, toward what is beyond that which had appeared in him corresponding to his capacity; for knowledge has a vastness which is not compatible with any narrowness [that is, cannot be confined within the limitations

102

of the one who seeks it, but transforms him]. So when He manifests to His servant in revelation, it prepares the servant for yet another revelation; and this is so endlessly. So satiation is unimaginable in the perfect lover of the Real, and limitation and ending are inconceivable for the receiver of revelation. Of this the shaykh said: "It is as if the experience of the one who is aware enters his heart through He Whose being is infinite, imposing a finiteness upon him for the sake of the manifestation thus made possible in him" which is *"beyond appearances. For the Apparent One, though He is one in essence, is infinite in aspects. They are His traces in us."* His attributes are not completed except in us. So we give Him the attributes, and He gives us being. And if the attainment of what is beyond this has no limit, it is because each contemplation results in bringing one face to face with a contemplation still more exalted. And thus it is without end.

"And for the like of this let the workers work, and for the like of this let the contenders contend...."

GLOSSARY

Abu-'Iqal al-Maghribi   A Sufi of the late eleventh century who
lived in Mecca for four years without eating or drinking, in
a state of *ghayba* (q.v.), lost to the world.

Abu-Yazid Bistami   Abu-Yazid Tayfur ibn 'Isa al-Bistami (d.
848 or 874), a great Sufi famous for ecstasy and mystical
traveling in reality. Grandson of a Zoroastrian, when
asked, "How did you find wisdom?" he replied, "by
hunger and poverty." He meditated for thirty years, and
was one of those who memorized the Koran. Once he took
his son to see a well known saint of the time. He saw the
man spit in the direction of the Kaaba. He took his son and
left immediately, saying, "How could anyone follow a man
who does not obey the *adab* of the Prophet (peace and
blessings be upon him)?" He said that he could not put into
words the greatest difficulty he had encountered on the
spiritual path, but the easiest he remembered was that once
when his *nafs* (q.v.) refused to make prayers, he punished it
by not drinking water for a year. Shaykh Musa ibn 'Isa
relates from his father that Hazrat Bistami said: "If you see

a man sitting crosslegged in the air but you learn that he doesn't totally follow the Sacred Law, don't believe in him.''

adab Etiquette, behavior; in Sufism, the mode of right action, the spiritual courtesy of the Way.

ahadiyya The Indivisible Unity of Allah, known only to Himself and those who are not other than He.

'alim Knower; in its general use, any learned man, particularly a theologian. Here, for Ibn 'Arabi, a master to whom Allah has assigned the task of teaching and guidance, following the Prophetic tradition ''The knowers are the inheritors of the prophets.''

'arif Gnostic, one who has become acquainted with the Divine Being. Here, for Ibn 'Arabi, particularly one who has no responsibility to the Creation, but only to the Creator.

asma' ilahiyya Divine Names, as mentioned in Koran 20:8: ''His are the most beautiful Names'' (*al-asma' al-husna*). The Divine Names are divided into Names of Essence, expressing pure transcendence, and Names of Attributes, expressing divine qualities and actions. Singular: *ism ilahi.*

'ayn Eye, but also the very self, as for instance in the term *'ayn al-yaqin,* eye of certainty, which means knowledge seen, but also the very reality of knowledge.

baqa' The installation of all the good attributes in man; eternal existence. (See *fana'.*) *Baqa'* is the beginning of traveling in God.

GLOSSARY

barzakh Interval; any intermediate state between two degrees of existence, especially the world of subtle forms between the physical and supraformal worlds.

dhikr Remembering, mention; the recollection of Allah through the invocation of His Names.

fana' The total disappearance of the bad attributes from man, annihilation; as implied in Koran 55:26-27: "Everything that is upon [the earth] vanishes; the face of your Lord remains in majesty and honor." (See *baqa'*.) *Fana'* is the end of traveling to God.

Fusus al-hikam "Bezels of Wisdom," Ibn 'Arabi's discussion of the Prophetic Words, the unique varieties of perfection realized in each of the 27 major prophets.

al-Futuhat al-Makkiyya "The Meccan Revelations" (so called because the angel of inspiration first appeared to him in Mecca to announce this work), Ibn 'Arabi's largest book, consisting of 560 chapters. It is a collection of teachings and observations on a vast variety of subjects.

ghayba Absence; the state of being unconscious of the world. Absence from the world implies presence with something else.

hadith Narration, account; report of the actions and sayings of the Prophet (peace be upon him) transmitted through trustworthy intermediaries. The Prophet said regarding hadith, "The faithful looks with the *nur* [light] of Allah." "The believers look with an *'ilm* [knowledge] and *basira* [insight] specially given only to them." *Nur* in this case means *'ilm* and *basira*. A "tradition" of the Prophet only becomes hadith when viewed with *'ilm* and *basira*, a gift of Allah to the believer.

hadith qudsi Sacred account; a non-Koranic Divine Word revealed through the Prophet (peace be upon him).

hadra Presence; one of the modes or levels of the Divine Presence. There are five major *hadarat:*

Hadrat ul-ghayb il-mutlaq, absolute nonmanifestation, reflected in the eternal fixed essences

Hadrat ul-ghayb il-mudaf, relative nonmanifestation, reflected in the universe of spirits

Hadrat ul-mithal, relative manifestation, reflected in the subtle forms

hadrat ul-mushahadat il-mutlaqa, absolute manifestation, reflected in the physical world

hadrat ul-jami'a, the presence of the totality, reflected in the Perfect Man

hafira Beginning; original state. See Koran 79:10: "They say: Shall we indeed be returned to the original state (*hafira*)?"

haqq Truth, the Real; the Divine Reality as distinguished from Creation. (See *khalq*.)

himma Resolution, determination, ardor; for Ibn 'Arabi, the spiritual will, the concentrated power of the heart's intention.

huwiyya From the pronoun *huwa*, "He": the ineffable Divine Identity; God Himself transcending attribute or description.

GLOSSARY

Ibn Jawziya   Shamsuddin Muhammad ibn Abu-Bakr al-Jawziya (1295-1356), a theologian and follower of Ibn Taymiyya, fundamentalist preacher and writer.

Ibn Rushd   Abul Walid Muhammad ibn Ahmad ibn Rushd (1126-1198), known also as Averroës, the greatest Arab philosopher of Spain, noted for his commentaries on Plato and Aristotle and his perceptive analysis. He was attacked as a heretic by contemporary theologians.

'ilm   Knowledge, science. *'ilm* is a light from the lamp of prophecy in the heart of the servant through which he finds the path to God, to the work of God, and to the order of God. *'Ilm* is the special characteristic of the human being; it refers neither to the understanding of the senses nor to reason. Intellect is that which discriminates between good and evil. The intellect which distinguishes the good and evil of this world belongs to believers and unbelievers alike. The intellect which distinguishes the good and evil of the next world belongs only to the believers. *'Ilm* is special to the believers; *'ilm* and true intellect are necessary to each other. The *knowledge* of certainty (*'ilm al'yaqin*) is to hear that fire exists. The *vision* of certainty (*'ayn al-yaqin*) is to see it yourself. But the *reality* of certainty (*haqq al-yaqin*) is to *be* fire.

istihlak   Absorption; for Ibn 'Arabi, the state of being consumed or overwhelmed by the Divine Presence so that all consciousness of multiplicity and the relative world is destroyed.

GLOSSARY

ithbat   Affirmation; here, the affirmation of what God has ordained. (See *mahw*.)

khala'   Void; according to Ibn 'Arabi, the state of the universe before its creation, and the origin of the word *khalwa* (q.v.).

khalq   Creation; the created world as differentiated from absolute reality. (See *haqq*.)

khalq jadid   Renewed creation. From Koran 50:14; "They are illusioned by a new creation." For Ibn 'Arabi, the instant-by-instant destruction and re-creation of the world which is the infinite manifestation of Allah.

khalwa   Retreat; the act of total abandonment in desire of the Divine Presence. The one who undertakes *khalwa*, like a dead man, surrenders all worldly and exterior religious affairs, as the first step to surrendering his own existence. In complete seclusion he continuously repeats the Name of God. A man was asked if he was a priest. He replied, "I am a guardian of dogs, seeing that they don't bite people, who may then live in peace and security. I locked up the dogs of my *nafs,* and am guarding them."

lawa'ih   Outward appearance, looks, signs. A state (*hal*), if not continuous, is called *lawa'ih* or *bada'ih*—that is, an isolated state. The occasionally appearing state of enlightenment in novices is *lawa'ih.* Of *lawa'ih,* a poet says, "O bright lightning, which part of heaven are you illuminating now?"

lawa'ih lawhiyya   "Surface signs" or "outward appearances of the Tablet." This expression of Ibn 'Arabi's is obscure. Jili identifies it with *lawa'ih haliyya* (see *lawa'ih*). Possibly the term derives from *al-lawh al-mahfuz*, the Guarded Tablet in which all destinies are written, identical with the Throne of Mercy (see *sarir al-rahmaniyya*). In the text, however, the Tablet is revealed at a much higher level than are these "surface signs."

mahq Obliteration; the unchanging state of not being able to see even one's self. It is the state above *mahw* (q.v.), for in the state of *mahw* traces remain, while in the state of *mahq* no traces remain. Jili states that it is the manifestation of the vice-regency of God and that its perfection does not belong to this world.

mahq al-mahq Obliteration of obliteration; the concealment of the vice-regency destined by Allah to the true human being. Jili states that *mahq al-mahq* may be perfected in this world.

mahw The elimination of one's habits (habitual attributes); it corresponds to *ithbat* (q.v.), action from the necessities of worship. *Mahw* means the erasure of errors from the visible self, of unconsciousness from the heart, and of the tendency to see other than Allah from the soul. *Mahw* is what God by His Will hides and eliminates; *ithbat* is what He reveals and makes existent. If one leaves one's habits, a product of one's own doing, and replaces them with the wondrous attributes and states, gifts, and returns granted through the worship of Allah, then one has the qualities of *mahw* and *ithbat*.

111

GLOSSARY

makr   Plot, ruse. The ruse of Allah is blessings which follow infringement of the Law, continuation of a state despite violation of *adab*, and the appearance of miracles without spiritual effort.

Malamiyya or *Malamatiyya*   Those Sufis whose discipline is to take blame upon themselves, accepting the world's attribution of guilt while remaining secretly innocent. Ibn 'Arabi applies this term to the highest grade of Sufis, who embody the secret of Muhammad (peace be upon him). Singular: *Malami* or *Malamati*.

maqam   A stage or level of spiritual development.

mardudun   Those sent back; Ibn 'Arabi's term for those who, having attained the Presence of Allah, are returned by Him to His creation. All else being equal, they are counted as superior to those who remain in exclusive contemplation. (See *mustahlikun*.) Singular: *mardud*.

mawatin   Realms; Ibn 'Arabi's term for the ultimate grounds or "homelands" of all created experience. They are six in number: pre-Creation, this world, the subtle world, Resurrection, Hell/Paradise, and the site of the Divine Vision "outside of Paradise." Singular: *mawtin*.

Muhibbuddin al-Tabari   Muhibbuddin Abul-'Abbas Ahmad ibn 'Abdullah al-Tabari (1218-1295), a traditionist and jurist in Mecca, the author of a well-known collection of hadith and 216 other surviving works.

Muhyiddin 'Abdul-Qadir Jilani   Muhyiddin Abu-Muhammad 'Abdul-Qadir ibn Abu-Salih al-Jilani Zengi Dost (1077-

GLOSSARY

1166), a saint of immense prestige and spiritual grace. Multitudes of legends and stories surround him. Trained first as a jurist, he became a Sufi at the hands of Shaykh Abul-Khayr Muhammad ibn Muslim al-Dabbas, who is said to have brought him to Sufism by a single glance. Shaykh 'Abdul-Qadir Jilani started to preach publicly in Baghdad in 1127. He rapidly became renowned as the most moving and eloquent of speakers and addressed vast audiences. He answered questions sent to him from all over the world and distributed huge amounts of charity. His spiritual status was such that he once stated, "My foot is on the neck of every saint." Many teachers of the highest caliber, in his own time and ever since, have acknowledged him as their master.

mustahlikun   Ibn 'Arabi's expression for those lost in the contemplation of God's Unity to the exclusion of His manifestation in multiplicity. (See *istihlak.*) Their state is not so high as the state of those who encompass both aspects. (See *mardudun.*) Singular: *mustahlik.*

al-nafas al-rahmani   The Merciful Breath; the Divine Mercy which "breathes out" the existence of the world.

nafs   Self, ego, desires. It is said that there is no approach to God except by God, and there is no veil between the servant and his Lord except his *nafs.* Sufism recognizes seven stages of refinement of the *nafs.*

al-Nuni   The one shaped like the letter *nun;* the name of an angel, the personification of the First Intellect in its passive aspect as the container of all knowledges.

GLOSSARY

qabd Contraction, closing. In Sufism, diminution of self by
withdrawing from the surface personality toward the
interior. As a stage, it describes the Sufi who has passed
beyond *khawf* (fear of Allah) and *raja'* (hope). At that level
khawf becomes *qabd; raja'* becomes *bast,* expansion. *Khawf*
and *raja'* pertain to the future, while *qabd* is the fear of now
and *bast* is the hope of now.

al-Qalam The Pen, title of the Seventieth Sura. It is the
Koranic term for the primordial comprehensive active
divine consciousness. The parallel philosophical expression, used by Ibn 'Arabi, is the First Intellect.

qutb Axis or pivot; the highest station in the Sufi hierarchy of
saints. The *qutb* is directly responsible for the welfare of the
entire world. The *qutb* is said to be the spiritual successor of
Muhammad.

al-Rabb Divine Name, the Lord. The Arabic implies the
cherisher, the one who guides the development of
something. Ibn 'Arabi says that this name rules the Cloud,
the primordial entity within which all conditions form.

al-Rahman Divine Name, the Merciful. The Mercy indicated
by this Name is that compassion which enfolds the whole
universe, and through which the universe was created. Ibn
'Arabi states that this Name rules the Throne of Mercy.
(See *sarir al-rahmaniyya.*)

riyada Training of character through ascetic practices.

Sa'duddin Hamawi Sa'ddudin Muhammad ibn al-Mu'ayad al-
Hamawi (1191 or '98-1252 or '60) was one of the twelve

GLOSSARY

inheritors of the great Shaykh Najmuddin Kubra, and a famous Sufi of his time. Sadruddin Qunyawi, the disciple of Ibn 'Arabi, attended his gatherings as a young man. Shaykh Hamawi was known as a composer of mystical poetry and Sufi texts. Many miracles are attributed to him. His soul is said to have once left his body for thirteen days.

sarir al-rahmaniyya The Throne of Mercy, called also the Guarded Tablet, is the Soul of the Universe. Every destiny and every knowledge are encompassed by it.

al-Sattar Divine Name, the Veiler (Who covers human sins).

shahwa Craving, natural appetite.

shaykh Master, spiritual guide, literally, "old man." The title of a teacher of Sufism (Also spelled *Sheikh*).

sura Form, whether physical, subtle, or abstract.

taklif The obligation of a human being to choose the service of God. Called by Ibn 'Arabi a constituting principle of this world.

tawali' Ascendant stars. In the course of development they follow the *lawa'ih* (q.v.). The *tawali'* are the first hints of the Divine Names which illuminate the servant and beautify his character. These are the lights of *tawhid* which overpower all lesser lights.

tawhid The declaration of the Unity of God expressed by the phrase *La ilaha ila 'llah,* "There is no god but God."

'ubudiyya The quality of the servant, said to be perfected in Muhammad (peace be upon him).

'Uqlat al-mustawfiz "The Spell of the Obedient Servant,"

115

a book by Ibn 'Arabi quoted by Jili. It concerns the Perfect Man and the degrees of being, and was written when Ibn 'Arabi was in his twenties or early thirties, before his pilgrimage to Mecca.

waqif   One who stops. Ibn 'Arabi uses this term for the seeker at the time that he reaches his object, whether that seeker then remains in contemplation (see *mustahlikun*) or returns to the world (see *mardudun*).

waqt   Moment; in Sufism, the duration of an episode of real conscious existence, of remembrance of Allah.

watan   Homeland, from the same root as *mawatin* (q.v.), Realm.